The Q Guide to Charlie's Angels

The Q Guides

FROM ALYSON BOOKS

AVAILABLE NOW:

THE Q GUIDE TO THE GOLDEN GIRLS
by Jim Colucci

THE Q GUIDE TO SOAP OPERAS
by Daniel R. Coleridge

THE Q GUIDE TO BROADWAY
by Seth Rudetsky

THE Q GUIDE TO OSCAR PARTIES
(AND OTHER AWARD SHOWS)
by Joel Perry

THE Q GUIDE TO FIRE ISLAND
by Steve Weinstein

THE Q GUIDE TO AMSTERDAM
by Dara Colwell

THE Q GUIDE TO NYC PRIDE
by Patrick Hinds

THE Q GUIDE TO WINE AND COCKTAILS
by Scott & Scott

THE Q GUIDE TO CLASSIC MONSTER MOVIES
by Douglas McEwan

THE Q GUIDE TO DESIGNING WOMEN
by Allen Crowe

THE Q GUIDE TO GAY BEACHES
by David Allyn

THE Q GUIDE TO BUFFY THE VAMPIRE SLAYER
by Gregory L. Norris

THE Q GUIDE TO SEX AND THE CITY
by Robb Pearlman

The Q Guide to Charlie's Angels

Stuff You Didn't Even Know You Wanted to Know . . . about three little girls who went to the police academy

[**Mike Pingel**]

[**Foreword by Tanya Roberts**]

To my mother and father, who never really understood my love affair with Charlie's Angels, *but nevertheless love me unconditionally! I love you both so much and thank you for all your support.*

MANUFACTURED IN THE UNITED STATES OF AMERICA

PUBLISHED BY ALYSON BOOKS
245 WEST 17TH STREET,
NEW YORK, NY 10011

DISTRIBUTION IN THE UNITED KINGDOM BY
TURNAROUND PUBLISHER SERVICES LTD.
UNIT 3, OLYMPIA TRADING ESTATE
COBURG ROAD, WOOD GREEN
LONDON N22 6TZ ENGLAND

FIRST EDITION: JULY 2008

08 09 10 11 12 13 14 15 16 17 a 10 9 8 7 6 5 4 3 2 1

ISBN: 1-59350-057-2
ISBN-13: 978-1-59350-057-3

LIBRARY OF CONGRESS CATALOGING-IN-PUBLICATION DATA ARE ON FILE.

COVER DESIGN BY VICTOR MINGOVITS

Contents

Author Mike Pingel with "Charlie's Angels" (from left to right and top to bottom) Farrah Fawcett, Cheryl Ladd, Kate Jackson and Jaclyn Smith, Shelley Hack and Tanya Roberts. (© Mike Pingel)

Foreword

CHARLIE'S ANGELS changed my life overnight. One day I was just a normal person, and then the next minute I'm on magazine covers around the world. It was crazy.

I enjoyed playing Julie Rogers. She was a bad-ass crime fighter with a heart of gold. To this day, she is one of my favorite characters.

I had such a blast working with Cheryl and Jaclyn. We had so much fun filming the show. They were such giving actors, and they really took care of me. Good old Boz, David Doyle, was always giving me helpful hints on the set. And to this day Aaron Spelling and "Cubby" Broccoli, the producer of my Bond film, remain the two kindest and most generous producers I have ever worked for.

I was just very happy to be there, loving it and having a good time. The first scene I ever shot was coming into the office at the end of my first show when they ask Julie, "Do you want to join us and be an Angel?" It was so weird: being asked to join the Angels on the air mirrored my real life as I was asked to join the cast of *Charlie's Angels.*

When I look back at the series, the funniest memory I have was the evening we were shooting "Hula Angels." Cheryl, Jaclyn, and I were getting a bit tired, and we couldn't get through the last scene of the night. David Doyle was standing quietly by the camera, and all of a sudden he turned around, dropped his pants, and mooned us all! We all broke out laughing.

I always thought *Charlie's Angels* was a cutting-edge show that could have gone on forever, and in this day and age it would have. How can one beat three hot chicks running around in couture fashions solving crimes every week?

Today it's still great to be a part of a series that everyone loves so much. I always smile when someone tells me that I was their favorite Angel. I hope you enjoy this fun look at *Charlie's Angels*.

—Tanya Roberts, January 2008

Introduction

ONCE UPON a time there was a little boy who loved TV. He watched everything he could—*The Six Million Dollar Man, Happy Days, One Day at a Time, Wonder Woman, Three's Company*—and the list goes on from there. Then one fateful Wednesday night, September 14, 1977, to be exact, he tuned into his first episode of *Charlie's Angels.* That night the newest Angel, Kris Munroe (Cheryl Ladd), had just arrived at the Townsend Agency. The Angels' beauty and the excitement of them going undercover hypnotized him right from the start. Thus began a lifelong love affair with the crime-fighting, gun-toting, and drop-dead-gorgeous Angels. I still get chills whenever I watch the opening credits of that particular show ("Angels in Paradise").

Fast forward fifteen years later. I created the newsletter titled *Angelic Heaven,* which became the basis for my website, CharliesAngels.com. The media came knocking on my door for interviews, along with my expertise and insight into a show that millions still love to this day.

In 1996, my ultimate dream came true. I finally met my very first and all-time-favorite Angel, Cheryl Ladd. She was doing a book signing for her children's book, *The Adventures of Little Nettie Windship.* It took almost twenty minutes to get up my nerve to go talk to her. Too bad the bookstore didn't serve alcohol because a gin and tonic would have helped to calm my nerves. Finally I went up and began chatting with Ladd. She could not have been nicer, and from there a friendship has blossomed. I now maintain Cheryl Ladd's official website (www.cherylladd.com), but to this day, whenever I talk with her, butterflies reappear in my stomach and I still get tongue-tied! That little boy is always there, and her heavenly voice always takes me back to that night in 1977. Over the next several years I would eventually meet the remaining Angels: Farrah Fawcett, Kate Jackson, Jaclyn Smith, Shelley Hack, and Tanya Roberts. All were equally as nice and just as sweet as Cheryl Ladd.

In early 2005, Farrah Fawcett began filming her reality series, *Chasing Farrah,* for TV Land. Farrah was looking for an assistant, and I was ready to become her co-Angel in crime. When I went in to be interviewed, the interview was also being filmed for her series. However, I made one disastrous mistake during the process. When her agent asked me who my favorite Angel was, I said without thinking, "Cheryl Ladd." Oops! Needless to say, I wasn't hired.

By late 2005, I received a phone call from Craig Nevis, who produced and directed *Chasing Farrah*. Farrah had wanted to come over to my apartment to see my *Charlie's Angels* collection. Without hesitation, I said yes. Next thing I knew, Farrah was in my apartment playing with my *Charlie's Angels* toys! Nevis noticed how well I interacted with Farrah and thought I would fit in perfectly as her assistant. A couple of weeks later, this Angel reported for duty. We would be working on films, photo shoots, and TV appearances together. I was in heaven!

In August 2006, a second dream came to fruition. I had always wished I could go back in time and be on the set of *Charlie's Angels,* and I got that opportunity. I was backstage at the Emmy Awards as Farrah Fawcett, Kate Jackson, and Jaclyn Smith reunited to pay tribute to the late, great Aaron Spelling. They looked as if they had just walked off the set of *Charlie's Angels.* I was so blessed that they allowed me to share in the joy and celebration of their reunion. That was an evening I will never forget.

I have always believed in fate and that God sends you where you need to go. There was a reason I was hired as Farrah Fawcett's assistant, other than the obvious. Shortly after the Emmy Awards, Farrah was diagnosed with cancer and faced the scary reality of doctors, chemotherapy, and tears. I was able to help her through the most devastating time of her life. One thing I learned about this Texas girl is that she is a fighter and one strong woman.

As I reflect back to the one Wednesday night in September 1977, who would have ever imaged how a TV show was going to totally change my life, let alone that one day I would work for both Cheryl Ladd and Farrah Fawcett? I hope this Q Guide gives you a fun insight into the show that I have loved so much. And remember, there is a little bit of the Angels inside all of us!

Got to run . . . the phone is ringing. It's Charlie calling me in for my newest assignment!

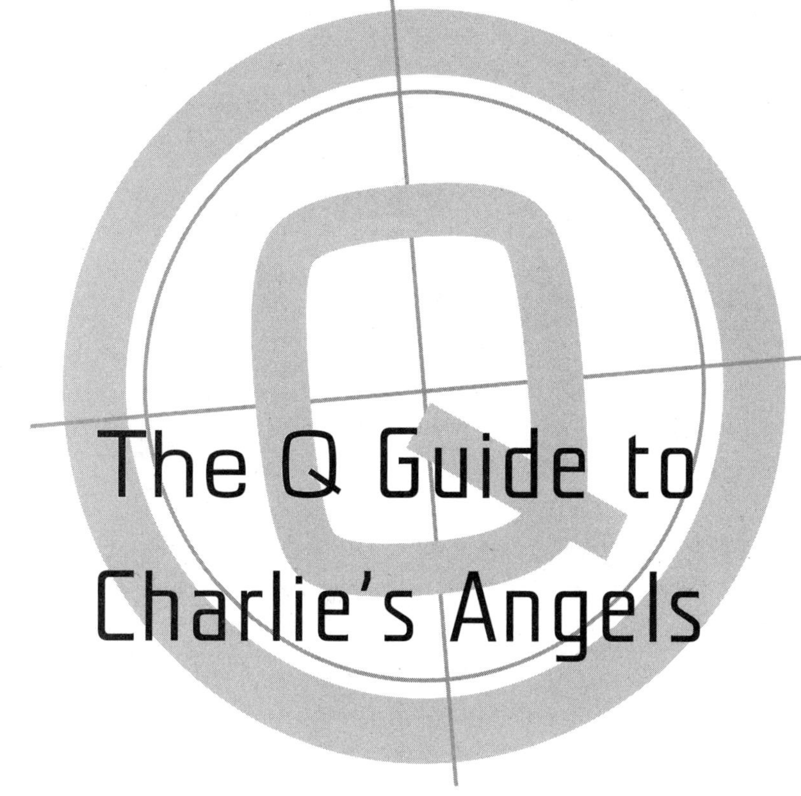

The Q Guide to Charlie's Angels

Jaclyn Smith, Kate Jackson, and Farrah Fawcett in the now-world-famous praying hand pose as Charlie's Angels. (© American Broadcasting Companies, Inc.)

CHAPTER ONE

Guardian Angels: History of the Wings

IT WAS the 1970s; disco balls and bell-bottoms were all the rage. Producers Aaron Spelling and Leonard Goldberg recognized a trend on TV on how women were breaking out of the typical housewife stereotypes. Sexy Angie Dickinson was arresting the airwaves in *Police Woman* over on NBC, independent woman Mary Tyler Moore was making everyone laugh on CBS, and *Maude* featured the first outspoken, opinionated female. The producers had a great idea about three female detectives, Alley, Lee, and Catherine, who fight crime on the streets of Los Angeles in leather. It would be called *The Alley Cats.*

Spelling and Goldberg pitched their idea to ABC executives during a breakfast meeting at the Beverly Hills Hotel. The executives thought it was the worst idea ever and passed on the show. However, they sold to ABC their new wholesome show called *Family,* which would focus on family problems and would star Kristy McNichol.

HEAVENLY TIDBITS: The 1970s

Angie Dickinson was nominated for an Emmy three times for her work in *Police Woman.* Mary Tyler Moore received eight Emmy nominations for *The Mary Tyler Moore Show.* She won four times for Outstanding Lead Actress in a Comedy Series, in 1973, twice in 1974 (the second one was for "Actress of the Year"), and in 1976. In 1977 Beatrice Arthur won the Emmy for Outstanding Lead Actress in a Comedy Series for her work in *Maude.* She received five more nominations for her work on the series.

Do you remember Kristy McNichol and her brother Jimmy singing "He's So Fine"? Their single, from their self-titled LP *Kristy and Jimmy McNichol,* reached number 70 on the music charts in 1978.

The French Connection, starring Gene Hackman and Roy Scheider, grossed $51 million in 1971. The film won five Academy Awards, including Best Picture, Best Actor for Hackman, and Best Screenplay for Ernest Tidyman.

Spelling and Goldberg never forgot about the *The Alley Cats.* A guardian angel showed up in the form of an old contract for a TV film called *The Affair,* which starred Robert Wagner and Natalie Wood. The contract included a development deal for a new TV series for Wagner. The "play or pay" deal meant that a series needed to be created for the star, or ABC would pay the producers a sum of money to create one.

Goldberg re-pitched to ABC executive Michael Eisner (who later headed the Walt Disney Company) the idea of letting them taking the money to get a script written for *The Alley Cats.* Eisner agreed, and a script was on its way to being written. Spelling and Goldberg offered Wagner and his wife, Natalie Wood, 45 percent of the shows revenues and positions as silent partners.

The producers hired Oscar-winner Ernest Tidyman, who had written the screenplay *The French Connection,* to pen the first pilot script for *The Alley Cats.* After submitting the script to ABC, the top brass shelved the idea, leaving *The Alley Cats* spayed once again.

It was not until Fred Silverman became the head of ABC programming that *The Alley Cats* began its ninth life. Silverman had moved over from CBS, where he had made the network number 1 with shows like *Maude, The Mary Tyler Moore Show,* and *Rhoda.* When he came on board at ABC in 1975, he saw *The Alley Cats* as a great platform for women viewers and gave a green light for a pilot film to be shot.

The producers felt that the show would be a great star vehicle for actress Kate Jackson. Jackson was costarring on the producers series hit, *The Rookies.* She was invited in for a brainstorming session at producer's office. Spelling and Goldberg told Jackson their original idea for *The Alley Cats.* Jackson's creative mind quickly went to work. She came up with the idea of the girls being detectives. As she looked around the room, she spotted on Spelling's desk a speakerphone and thought they should work for a guy they never saw named "Harry" and he would give them instructions over the phone. Everyone liked the idea, but Jackson was still not

Jaclyn Smith and Kate Jackson have a laugh while taking a break from filming "Angel Trap." (© catrescue@monmouth .com/Nancy Barr-Brandon)

happy about the title. She looked above Spelling's head and there hung a painting of three angels, and it came to Jackson: "Angels! We should call them 'Harry's Angels'!" And the series was born.

When Spelling and Goldberg presented their new idea to Fred Silverman, he liked what he heard and suggested the writing team of Ivan Goff and Ben Roberts to bring all the ideas that Spelling and Goldberg and Jackson had created during their brainstorming session into a TV pilot script. Silverman had worked with those writers at CBS, where they created the hit show *Maxim*. Goff and Roberts created the world of

HEAVENLY TIDBITS

Kate Jackson played Nurse Danko on the Spelling-Goldberg series *The Rookies,* which centered around rookie police officers on the streets of Los Angeles. Jackson re-teamed with her TV husband Sam Melville, who had played her ex-husband Joe King on *Scarecrow and Mrs. King.* She also worked with another *Rookies* costar, Michael Ontkean, in the 20th Century Fox film *Making Love,* one of the first-ever gay mainstream motion pictures. Her third costar, Georg Stanford Brown, went on to direct eight episodes of *Charlie's Angels.* Brown also won two Emmy awards—one for directing a *Cagney & Lacey* episode in 1986, and for his work in *Roots* in 1977.

Harry's Angels with basic story arcs and three heavenly Angels named Sabrina Duncan, Jill Munroe, and Kelly Garrett.

With Jackson on board, the producers wanted a cast a blonde. They decided to ask Farrah Fawcett, the wife of actor Lee Majors. Majors played Colonel Steve Austin on the ABC-TV hit series *The Six Million Dollar Man.* Fawcett had made several guest appearances on the show. She had also made three TV movies for Spelling and Goldberg, *The Girl Who Came Gift Wrapped, Murder on Flight 501,* and *The Great American Beauty Contest.* Fawcett accepted the role, and then the focus turned to finding the third Angel.

For the last Angel, the producers wanted a redhead. Many actresses were considered for the role, including Priscilla Presley, Lynda Carter, Loni Anderson, and front-runner Veronica Hamel. Hamel decided not to take the part because she was looking for grittier roles and didn't want to be known as pretty face. Then Robert

HEAVENLY TIDBITS

Farrah Fawcett and Loni Anderson played battling beauties in the 1975 episode of *S.W.A.T.* entitled "Steel-Plated Security Blanket." And in 1976, Farrah Fawcett and Lynda Carter were teammates for ABC, competing against NBC and CBS in the very first *Battle of the Network Stars.*

HEAVENLY TIDBITS

Jaclyn Smith played a reoccurring character on Robert Wagner's 1975 TV series, *Switch*. The two teamed together again for the 1988 TV movie, *Windmills of the Gods*, and then for a third time in 2006 on ABC's *Hope & Faith*, in which Smith played Wagner's love interest.

Wagner suggested that Spelling and Goldberg audition a young actress named Jaclyn Smith, with whom he had worked on his TV series *Switch*.

After a handful of auditions, Smith finally read with Jackson and Fawcett. The producers and their two Angels thought Smith would be a perfect fit as Harry's third Angel.

HEAVENLY NOTE

Cheryl Ladd also guest-starred in an episode of *Switch*, and she played Wagner's deceased wife on *Hope & Faith*!

HEAVENLY TIDBITS

Lynda Carter was one of the producers' top picks to be an Angel. However, she was under contract with Warner Brothers at the time for *Wonder Woman*.

Next up, Spelling and Goldberg needed to hire the two men who would help out the Angels. First was Scott Woodville, the agency's lawyer; that role was given to David Ogden Stiers. And David Doyle was cast as John Bosley, the office manager.

With the cast set, filming began. The show centered around three female detectives hired to find a missing vineyard owner. After reading the script, Kate Jackson found the role of Sabrina Duncan more appealing than the role of Kelly Garrett that she was set to play. The pilot film was written to focus on Jackson's character Kelly. The role was then given to Jaclyn Smith, which is the reason she had a much larger role than the other two Angels.

The only character not cast was the voice of Harry (Charlie Townsend). Oscar-winner Gig Young was originally cast, but he arrived at the voice taping too drunk to do the job. At the eleventh hour, Aaron Spelling frantically called in a late-night favor from his good friend John Forsythe to voice Charlie.

The show was still on shaky ground. After viewing the pilot, Fred Pierce, the President of ABC Television, wanted to know where these "Angels" came from. On

HEAVENLY TIDBITS

Actor Byron Elsworth Barr became Gig Young after he adopted the name from his role in the film *The Gay Sisters* in 1942. He went on to win the 1969 Oscar as Best Actor in a Supporting Role for *They Shoot Horses, Don't They? Bewitched* star Elizabeth Montgomery was Gig's third wife; they divorced in 1963. By 1978, he had married his fifth wife. Three weeks later, Gig shot his wife and then shot himself in a murder-suicide, and his Oscar was found lying between them.

the spot, Aaron Spelling made up the background story of the Angels graduating from the Police Academy and being hired by a man named Charlie. Pierce liked the concept, and it also would allow the Angels to use guns. The other update the pilot film received was a name change. Because another TV show was named *Harry O, Harry's Angels* was changed to *Charley's Angels*. Before it hit the airways, the title was updated again to *Charlie's Angels*.

The TV film was completed, but ABC still had no heavenly faith in the concept, especially after test audiences gave the TV film the worst feedback ever in ABC Television history. ABC executives decided to air the film with little promotion on March 21, 1976. The Nielsen ratings went through the roof, surprising everyone. It pulled in a 59 percent rating. At that time, only Superbowls would pull in that many viewers.

"Having just welcomed a baby girl into our family, I thought it would be important to have a series on television that would offer female heroes to the audience. And to make the point that women are equally as capable in the action-adventure arena which had heretofore been reserved for men."

—Producer Leonard Goldberg, on creating the show

ABC did some juggling to fit the Angels into the 1976 fall TV schedule. It pitted the show against NBC's *Blue Knight* and CBS's new series *The Quest*, which was getting a lot of industry buzz. Little did they know Angel power was on its way.

A few more changes were made to the show when it became a series. First, the role of Woodville, the companies' lawyer, was eliminated, and his duties were given to the Angels' buddy, John Bosley. Second, the girls would now be carrying guns, and finally, the Townsend Detective Agency building exterior was changed from a white building with pillars to a more classy brick building.

Kate, Farrah, and Jaclyn began filming their first episode, "The Killing Kind," in July 1976. They formed a southern bond because Farrah and Jaclyn were from Texas and Kate was from Alabama.

Kate Jackson arrived in Los Angeles a well-seasoned actor after her long run on the daytime soap *Dark Shadows.* In New York she had attended the Academy of Dramatic Arts and was a NBC page, giving guided tours of the NBC New York studio. After her nine months on *Dark Shadows,* Jackson found herself driving to Los Angeles, where she was cast in *Movin' In* and *The Jimmy Stewart Show.* She soon found herself working on the Spelling-Goldberg TV series *The Rookies,* which lasted for four years.

Farrah Fawcett was born in Corpus Christi, Texas, to Jim and Pauline Fawcett and had an older sister named Diane. Her career toward stardom began quite simply, as she dabbled in a few photo shoots, was active as a cheerleader, and fell in love with art while in college. But after a publicist saw her picture in the newspaper, Hollywood began to call this Angel almost every night. It was said that the girls in Farrah's dorm would yell down the hall, "Hollywood is calling." Finally, Farrah convinced her parents to bring her out to Hollywood after her sophomore year at the University of Texas. Soon after her arrival in Los Angeles, she signed a contract with Screen Gems. Her first film was *Love Is a*

Funny Thing, and she became the spokesperson for Mercury Cougar and Noxzema.

As the Breck girl, Jaclyn Smith learned how to sell a product and tell a story in thirty seconds. This dazzling beauty from Houston, Texas, was selling everything from English Leather to Camay soap. The youngest of two children of Jack and Margaret Ellen Smith, she learned that family always comes first. She studied ballet and eventually taught ballet to underprivileged children in New York. In New York she also met and married a young actor named Roger Davis. The couple moved to Los Angeles, where Smith landed parts in *McCloud* and *Switch.*

Before *Charlie's Angels* made it to the air, Wella Balsam had signed the Angels as spokeswomen for its product line. Farrah pitched Wella Balsam conditioner, Jaclyn did Wella Balsam shampoo, and Kate was a hit with Wella Kolestral.

Hair, makeup, and the hottest fashions from Paris were about to hit the small screen, and these three little girls were about to take the world by storm. But a clatter was already starting because of a poster Fawcett had shot before filming *Charlie's Angels.* It would eventually be known around the world as the "Red Bathing Suit" poster and would embody the spirit of the 1970s. A small company called Pro-Arts asked Farrah to pose for a poster, and she accepted. Then she and photographer Bruce McBroom went to his Hollywood home and began to shoot photos. During the final part of the shoot, Farrah put on a one-piece rust-colored swimsuit, and Bruce grabbed an old Mexican blanket from his truck. With a few clicks of the shutter, an icon was born.

This was one very smart icon. She controlled her image

"The success of the show was all happening around us, but I didn't have time to notice. They would come in and tell us the ratings. We got a 40 percent share and it was number 3. I thought it was the norm, but we literally could only enjoy it for a second because we were working so hard."

—Farrah Fawcett

and even had her contract written to specify that the copyright to her posters with Pro-Arts revert back to her after their contract expired. The poster was a money-maker maker, with over 12 million copies sold. Fawcett would go on to have seven posters released and would pocket millions for her winning smile and bouncy hair.

On the night of September 21, 1976, at 10 p.m. the unforgettable theme music played, showcasing three little girls doing very hazardous duties with Charlie taking them away from all that. That week the show came in at number 3 in the Neilson ratings, which was fantastic for a brand-new show. The following week it hit number 2 and subsequently went straight to number 1. The show's ratings never tapered off during that first season. Its final rating for the 1976–1977 season was number 4.

The show was a hit, and everyone wanted the Angels. Endorsement deals, magazine covers, and even being asked to sing and release their own *Charlie's Angels* record album. The album deal never materialized, but Spelling and Goldberg did start negotiating product deals with Hasbro, HG Toys, Fleetwood Toys, Revell, Bantam Books, and many others for various *Charlie's Angels* products.

Success brought the Angels much unwanted attention. Adoring fans sent thousands of letters daily, but there were some who began to obsess, Jaclyn Smith had a stalker, and there were rumors of kidnapping threats surrounding the actress.

The Angels were a hot commodity. They landed on

HEAVENLY TIDBITS

In 1975 Farrah Fawcett recorded a small 45 record with Jean Paul Vignon before the success of *Charlie's Angels.* The song was titled "You," with Fawcett singing/saying the lyrics. The single was only sold through mail order in 1977. In 2005, "You" was heard by millions of viewers on Fawcett's reality series, *Chasing Farrah.*

the cover of *People, TV Guide,* and even *Time* magazine for its feature story, "TV Super Women." The world's love affair with *Charlie's Angels* had just begun. The demand for the Angels was so big it began to take a toll on the set, with visitors holding up production. After seventeen episodes, the set was marked as a "closed set."

The Angels were getting industry nods. The series won Best New Series and Farrah Fawcett won for Best Actress at the 1977 People's Choice Awards. The show was nominated for three Emmys for the 1976–1977 season, including Kate Jackson for Outstanding Lead

Jaclyn Smith and Kate Jackson arrive at the 1977 People's Choice Awards, where the show took home the award for "Favorite Overall New TV Program," and Farrah won "Favorite Female Performer in a New TV Program." (©catrescue@monmouth.com/Nancy Barr-Brandon)

"During the first year the Angels were on the air, I received a call at the office from a man who said he represented the rulers of a Middle Eastern country and wanted to know how they could get *Charlie's Angels*. I told him that there was a company in charge of selling *Charlie's Angels* to the international markets and offered to give him the name of the man in charge and the number. After a bit of back and forth, I realized that the man was not interested in procuring the filmed episodes; he was literally inter-

> ested in the three Angels themselves. I gave him the telephone number of each of their agents and hung up just in time to burst out laughing."
>
> —Leonard Goldberg, producer

Actress in a Drama Series; David Doyle for Outstanding Continuing Performance as a Supporting Actor in a Dramatic Series, and episode 2, "The Mexican Connection," for Outstanding Achievement in Film Sound Editing. The Golden Globes also nominated the show for two categories for Best New Series—Drama, and Jackson and Fawcett both were up for Best Performance by an Actress in TV Series—Drama.

The production year was going smoothly until Farrah Fawcett announced that she was not returning to the hit show. The producers were shocked. On Friday, March 11, 1977, they filed suit in the Los Angeles Superior court against Fawcett, and the legal battle began. Fawcett had not signed her original contract because the amount she would be paid for the merchandise of *Charlie's Angels* had never been resolved. The producers claimed that Fawcett had a contract because she arrived at work every day.

Spelling and Goldberg blacklisted Fawcett by letting other studios know that if they hired her they, too, might be sucked into the $7 million lawsuit. Fawcett lost two upcoming feature film roles: the first one was the lead opposite Chevy Chase in the film *Foul Play,* which Goldie Hawn took over; and the second was the lead in *Coma,* which went to Genevieve Bujold. Both feature films went on to be hits in 1978.

On Thursday, April 7, 1977, it was announced that ABC-TV had renewed *Charlie's Angels* for a second season. The producers had to begin a search for a new Angel. If they could not get Fawcett to come back, who would fill in her bell-bottom blue jeans? Kim Basinger was the top-rumored actress in Hollywood to replace Fawcett. Basinger had guest-starred on the series the past year as the office secretary, but that role never materialized.

It was the stunning Cheryl Ladd that caught Aaron Spelling's eye once again. She had almost landed the role of Nancy on the producers' hit show *Family* and had filmed the TV movie, *Satan's School for Girls,* in which she costarred with Kate Jackson. Spelling had asked Ladd to come in for a screen test, and she turned him down. Time was running out, and the new season was about to begin shooting. It looked like Fawcett was not coming back. After seeing so many hopeful Angels, Spelling still felt Ladd was the right actress for the role. So he bit the bullet and told her he understood her reasons for not wanting to take the role but asked her to please come in for a meeting. Ladd accepted.

In Spelling's office, he and Ladd began creating another character who would hopefully be the answer to all his prayers. The twosome created Charlie's fourth Angel, Kris Munroe.

As Ladd's screen test, she was to film her first episode "Circus of Terror." On Ladd's first day of shooting during the first week of June 1977, she decided to break the ice by wearing a T-shirt that said "Farrah Fawcett–Minor." She made everyone laugh, and then the work began. After the show wrapped, the producers were so pleased with Ladd's performance that she was given her Angel role permanently. This was major news, a new Angel in town. The media were going berserk, twisting the stories around and saying the Angels were not getting along.

Even with Cheryl Ladd on board, the producers still hoped that Fawcett would return to work when the second season began. The filming of the second episode on Friday, June 10, 1977, was shut down by ABC-TV. They felt ramifications would occur if they continued to film the series. The next week, everything was ironed out, and the Angels flew to Hawaii to shoot "Angels in Paradise."

There were two major changes to *Charlie's Angels* that season: the introduction of new Angel Kris Munroe (Cheryl Ladd) and the movement of the show from 10 p.m. to 9 p.m., introducing the Angels to a wider audience.

On Wednesday, September 14, 1977, Kris Munroe walked into the Townsend Detective Agency and into million of viewers' living rooms. Everyone loved her. The ratings went up, and *Charlie's Angels* was flying high once again. Kris Munroe was a perfect match for the two remaining Angels. A sigh of relief was heard.

HEAVENLY TIDBITS

Farrah Fawcett replaced Cheryl Ladd in the lead role of *The Burning Bed* after Ladd turned it down. Fawcett played battered wife Francine Hughes, who murders her husband by pouring gasoline around his bed and striking a match to it while he's sleeping. Fawcett was nominated for an Emmy and a Golden Globe for her performance.

Spelling and Goldberg were delighted that Ladd was able to slip into Fawcett's bell-bottom jeans! It took some of the pressure off their lawsuit with Fawcett.

Soon after the second season began filming, Spelling and Goldberg went into court against Farrah Fawcett. The basis of their lawsuit was that Fawcett had arrived at work daily, so that even without a signed contact, she should be bound to her five-year contract. After a two-week court battle in April 1978, the two sides came to an agreement that Fawcett would return to the series for three episodes each year during the third and fourth seasons at a rumored salary of $150,000 per episode.

The filming of the second season's twenty-three episodes went by very quickly. Kate Jackson was once again nominated for an Emmy and a Golden Globe for her work as Sabrina, and the series was nominated for a Golden Globe. Yet the series did not win that year.

The Angels' love lives were talked about in those days just as Britney's, Paris's, and Lindsay's are today.

Fawcett was married to the Six Million Dollar Man, Lee Majors Jaclyn Smith married Dennis Cole in the fall of 1978. Cheryl Ladd was married to David Ladd and had a daughter named Jordan. And that summer, Kate Jackson married Andrew Stevens. The power couple also signed a very lucrative development deal with ABC. Their first project was a remake of the movie *Topper.*

In the summer of 1978, Kate Jackson and Dustin Hoffman held a press conference to announce their new feature film *Kramer vs. Kramer,* a story about a custody battle between a divorced couple. It was to be shot in New York during the winter. It was a great character departure for Jackson, and she was extremely excited about working on such a meaty role. But back in Hollywood, Spelling and Goldberg refused to let her out of her Angels schedule to film the feature. Jackson had to turn down the role and was devastated.

With season three filming beginning, Jackson was happy for the return of Farrah Fawcett to the series for her first three settlement episodes. In "Angel Come

HEAVENLY TIDBITS

Jaclyn Smith teamed up with husband Dennis Cole for the *Love Boat* episode "A Tasteful Affair," in which Smith plays a married woman who starts to fall for a private investigator (Cole) hired by her jealous husband, who believes she's having a torrid affair.

Home," Jill Munroe returns to Los Angeles after receiving a telegram from her little sister Kris. But Jackson's happy reunion with Fawcett was short-lived. Fawcett made her three guest appearances and returned to her life as a movie star.

After Kate Jackson was forced to let go of her role in *Kramer vs. Kramer,* the film went on to be a box-office winner and won an Oscar for Best Picture that year. Meryl Streep took over Jackson's role and won an Oscar

"People ask, Wasn't Charlie's Angels just a jiggle show? First of all, it was the first time there had been a show with three women leads. We had the roles that men would play. We were smart. We figured it out. We caught the bad guys. We were intelligent, and a lot of people got that."

—Farrah Fawcett

for Best Supporting Actress. This only fueled Jackson's desire to get out of her halo. The tabloids began to report that Jackson was a terror on the set and screamed about poorly written scripts. On May 15, 1979, ABC-TV announced that Kate Jackson had been let out of her contract and would not be returning to *Charlie's Angels* next season. Unlike Fawcett, Jackson's deal with the producers did not include her returning for any guest appearances.

The heavenly search was on again for another Angel. The major problem with Jackson leaving was that her character anchored the investigation team. Who could fill Sabrina's turtleneck? A parade of Angelic actresses strolled into Spelling and Goldberg's office, including Barbara Bach, Kelly Harmon, and Michelle Pfeiffer. Many magazines leaked the story that Barbara Bach, the future Mrs. Ringo Starr, who played Major Anya Amasova in the 1977 James Bond film *The Spy Who Loved Me,* had won the role of the newest Angel. Even though Bach won many magazine covers for the story, she did not win the replacement Angel role.

Going halo to halo for the coveted role of Angel Tiffany Welles were actresses Connie Sellecca and Shelley Hack. Connie Sellecca was a beautiful brunette who had just costarred on the CBS Angel copycat show *Flying High,* about three flight attendants who fight crime in the sky and on the ground. Shelley Hack was a classic blonde supermodel-turned-actress. She was also known around the world as Revlon's "Charlie Girl," promoting their signature fragrance, Charlie.

On May 30, 1979, Shelley Hack was handed her halo and was ready to set sail on her first Angelic adventure

CELEBRITY SURVEY #1: WHICH ANGEL ARE YOU AND WHY?

"I'm Sabrina. I'm the one always warning everyone of danger, and least likely to rely on my feminine charms to get out of a pinch."

—John August, screenwriter, *Charlie's Angels, Charlie's Angels: Full Throttle, Go*

"Definitely Sabrina. She may not be the prettiest one, but she's definitely the smartest—and the sassiest."

—Peter Paige, actor, *Queer as Folk*

"I'm Kelly, because of her long brown flowing hair, and I like to wear wigs."

—ANT, comedian, actor, *Last Comic Standing*

"Well, I went on to wear huge blonde hair and take drugs—I mean exhibit erratic behavior—so I'd have to pick Farrah."

—Lady Bunny, ladybunny.net

"If I were an Angel, it would have to be Sabrina because she was the more androgynous one. I had crushes on all the other Angels. I would have to say Sabrina. Definitely."

—Michelle Wolff, actress, *Dante's Cove*

"Isn't it obvious!? I'm Sabrina Duncan, of course! Why? Because I'm beautiful AND smart!"

—Jackie Beat, Jackiebeatrules.com

"I have to say Tanya Roberts. She was the bad girl in the first episode she was in, and they were actually chasing her. She was the one getting into trouble, and she turned and became one of the good girls. I love when bad girls become good girls"

—Chi Chi LaRue, porn director

"Since I'm a bit more of a leader, Sabrina. But I dress a bit more like Jill ("Giggling Tease")."

—Glen Hanson, artist of my HEAVENLY cover artwork!

"I remember that I collected the *Charlie's Angels* bubble gum cards (still have them!) and I usually traded out my Jaclyn Smith and my Cheryl Ladd for the Kate Jackson cards. That's because when I played *Charlie's Angels* with two of my girlfriends that lived on my block, I was *always* Kate Jackson . . . the sensible, kind of butch, one. I guess back then I had the clothes for it."

—Miss Coco Peru, actress, *Trick, Girls Will Be Girls*

"I had the Farrah poster on my bedroom wall growing up in New Jersey. In retrospect, I was just using her to get to Lee Majors. But even as a kid, when I watched *Charlie's Angels,* I always identified with Bosley. When I grew up and first moved to New York, I *was* Bosley—plump, fey, and constantly surrounded by beautiful women. Now that I do my radio show on Sirius every day, though, I feel more like Charlie. I've become a disembodied voice that tells people what to do."

—Frank DeCaro, host, *The Frank DeCaro Show* on Sirius

"I would have to say I'm Kelly Garrett. I would rather be Kelly because she's beautiful, smart, and has a successful line of clothes at KMart. How can you beat that?"

—Julie Brown, comedian, actress, and singer

"I'm Kris Munroe, because I'm crazy, perky, upbeat, and I have a winning personality."

—Dylan Vox, actor, *The Lair*

aboard *The Love Boat* en route to St. Thomas in the Caribbean, where the Angels don swimsuits while looking for $5 million in stolen antiques.

The media frenzy over Shelley Hack joining the cast was as big as Paris Hilton going to jail. Hack was found on hundreds of magazines covers and was an overnight celebrity. Just like Ladd, everyone was interested in Hack's likes and dislikes and her own sexy clothing style.

Charlie's Angels was always about the best of the best in style and fashion. Season four showcased the highest fashions with the addition of supermodel Shelley Hack. The fashion style they gave her character, Tiffany Welles, was ultra vogue. Nolan Miller, the show's costume designer, went wild dressing the Angels in tons of gowns, pantsuits, and furs.

HEAVENLY TIDBITS

Spelling sure has an eye for talent. Michelle Pfeiffer did not win the new Angel role, but Spelling put her under a development contract. She started with the short-lived show *B.A.D. Cats.* Pfeiffer went on to be one of Hollywood's sexiest leading ladies, starring in major hits such as *The Witches of Eastwick, Scarface, Dangerous Liaisons,* and most recently *Hairspray* and *Stardust.* Pfeiffer has been nominated for three Oscars and won a Golden Globe for *The Fabulous Baker Boys.* But don't forget that guilty musical pleasure, *Grease 2,* in which she played one of the kick-ass Pink Ladies!

Another major change on the series was the way the shows were being written. Smith and Ladd were getting a bit tired of the weekly grind of doing the series, so each episode primarily focused on one Angel. One week Kelly is becoming addicted to heroin ("Avenging Angels"), the next week Kris is sent to prison ("Caged Angel"), and the following week Tiffany goes back to college and gets kidnapped ("Angels on Campus"). Even though the shows were being written a bit differently, the show still had the same great "Angel" formula. Someone hires the Angels, they change clothes, go undercover, change clothes, get into jeopardy, change clothes, get rescued and solve the case, change clothes, and then recap the case while drinking cocktails.

The fourth season got a bad rap. The new Angel, Tiffany Welles, was not integrated into the group as well as

HEAVENLY TIDBITS

Spelling-Goldberg productions were trying to cut costs, so they had *Charlie's Angels* travel via *The Love Boat* set, instead of taking a real cruise ship to St. Thomas. "Love Boat Angels" (episode 69) won the Most Amazing Cast Cross-Over award on the 2003 TVLand awards. Who knew such a bad TV script idea could be so celebrated. That same year Charlie Townsend won Favorite "Heard But Not Seen" Character.

Cheryl Ladd's new character Kris had been two years earlier. Tiffany Welles's father was a close school friend of Charlie's, and she had just graduated from the Police Academy in Boston. The writers gave Tiffany a Boston background to bring a bit of sophistication and smarts to the character to compensate for the exit of Sabrina. But due to poorly written scripts, it worked against the character.

HEAVENLY TIDBITS

The year 1973 saw the introduction of Charlie fragrance, designed for a young, working woman market, and by the mid-1970s, Charlie was the number 1 fragrance in the world. Revlon sales figures passed the $1 billion mark in 1977.

HEAVENLY TIDBITS

In 2000, Shelley Hack and John Forsythe were co-hosts for A&E's *Biography* series, which presented features on Farrah Fawcett, Jaclyn Smith, Cheryl Ladd, John Forsythe, and Drew Barrymore.

The ratings for the series began to fall during the fourth season. It was also 1979, and TV was changing. New shows such as *Dallas, Dynasty* (produced by Aaron Spelling and Douglas S. Cramer), and *Flamingo Road* were beginning to rule television. Nighttime soap operas were upon us, and in the TV world, wealthy families began to take over as the rich and famous become richer and backstabbing and catfights dominated the television landscape. *Charlie's Angels* began to feel the slow death of the changing viewing audience. Even the new "classy" Angel and the glamour of Nolan Miller couldn't keep the audience coming back.

With ratings going down, the producers decided to let Shelley Hack go after only one season. Before she was informed of the release, it was reported that all the Angels except Hack were sent a Valentine's Day telegram inviting them back for another year. Hack did not know of her departure until the following day, when her press agent found out from a reporter. Even though she lost her halo and wings, there were three more shows for Hack to film, which included a two-part

"Yeah, eventually I just trusted them. I got bored with choosing it all and doing all those wardrobe fittings. Some of the outfits I chose, and some they chose for me. We were working so hard, I just wanted to get it done and go home to my baby."

—Cheryl Ladd, on Angel clothing

episode, "One Love . . . Two Angels," in which she took the reins as the lead Angel solving the crime.

Once again, a search went on for a new Angel. The producers hoped the search would increase visibility for the show and increase the lagging ratings. The new Angel selected was Tanya Roberts, who had a knockout body. Roberts's acting career was blossoming. She had done several movies, including *Zuma Beach* and *Tourist Trap*. Roberts had been cast in the rival CBS show "Flying High" but was let go after the series was retooled. In 1980, she had filmed a two-hour episode of *Vega$* titled "Golden Gate Cop Killer" for Spelling and Goldberg. It

HEAVENLY TIDBITS

Nolan Miller was one of the top designers of the TV landscape for women. He started his TV career by teaming up with Aaron Spelling in the 1970s. However, it was not until the hit series *Dynasty* that Miller was able to strut his distinct style of fashion for the very rich Carrington clan. Miller was nominated for five Emmys and won in 1993 for his work on *Dynasty.* He continues to design both clothing and jewelry for the very elite in Beverly Hills.

was to serve as a spin-off show called *Ladies in Blue,* costarring Michelle Phillips. The spin-off never got a green light, and she became the front-runner for the newest Angel. Roberts went up against Jayne Kennedy and Susie Coelho, then the wife of Sonny Bono.

On June 17, 1980, Tanya Roberts was announced to the press as the newest Angel. She had beaten out two

HEAVENLY TIDBITS

In 1979, Tanya Roberts was up for the lead role in the movie *10.*

thousand other hopeful actresses. But this girl from Brooklyn, New York, won the hearts of the producers. They hoped her rock-solid heavenly looks and spitfire attitude would boost the sagging ratings.

Then came a scandal, Spelling and Goldberg came under investigation for embezzling money from their silent partners, Natalie Wood and Robert Wagner. Jennifer Martin, an accountant at ABC, uncovered that the producers were skimming money from *Charlie's Angels* and filtering it through their other series *Starsky & Hutch*. The transfers were not detected until *Starsky & Hutch* had been canceled and the money had to be sent through the accounting department at *Charlie's Angels*. After the Los Angeles district attorney began looking into the allegations, "Angelgate" was quickly settled out of court.

Season five was ready to shoot in June 1980. Hoping

HEAVENLY TIDBITS

In July 2004, Robert Wagner brought a lawsuit against Sony Pictures for 50 percent of the profit from the two *Charlie's Angels* feature films on the basis of his involvement with the original series. He also sued Aaron Spelling Productions for a percentage of *Beverly Hills 90210*, based on the fact that the show was picked up after *Angels '88* was scrapped, from which he was to get 7.5 percent of the profits.

to bring in more viewers, the producers sent the Angels to Hawaii, giving them more opportunities to wear bikinis. As soon as the season got underway, the Screen Actors Guild went on strike. The Hawaiian production was shut down, and everyone headed back to the mainland. The strike ended in October, and the Angels went back to work, this time in Los Angeles. The new season premiered on a new night, Sunday, and at a new time, 8 p.m., on November 30, 1980. Due to sagging ratings, the Angels were moved to Saturday nights and were eventually pulled from the lineup in February 1981. The final four episodes aired in June 1981. After only eighteen episodes in 1980–1981, the Angels' wings were clipped, with official cancellation on July 18, 1981.

"Let Our Angel Live" was the final episode of the series. *Charlie's Angels* did not leave the airwaves with a bang—no full cast reunion or a fond farewell. The

"Jaclyn and Cheryl were tired of the show and knowing the end of the series was coming soon. I came at the end of the party"

—Tanya Roberts

show that blazed the trail for women in TV ended quietly on July 24, 1981. The Angels live on today in reruns around the world, DVD releases, and two hit feature films. Jackson, Fawcett, Smith, Ladd, Hack, and Roberts have left their legacy on the television landscape and will forever be remembered as Charlie's Angels.

On Cloud Nine with Farrah Fawcett

I guess I was the chosen one. At times it felt I was trying to seduce the speaker phone. They always had me saying lines like (in her sweet Jill voice again) "Well Charlie, if you want I can bring it over." At first I was really shy about it, but as the show went on I learned how to have fun with it—on acting to the speaker box.

How did you get your role on the series?

I had filmed the movie of the week, *Murder on Fight 502*, which was an ensemble piece with Ralph Bellamy, Polly Bergen, Walter Pidgeon, Brooke Adams and Robert Stack. That was the first time I did one of Aaron's shows. It was because of that footage he remembered me and sent me the script and asked if I would do *Charlie's Angels*.

Kate was already attached to the project, but it took a while, and many beautiful girls auditioned for the last role. Finally they called us in for a reading when they were deciding on Jaclyn. Our chemistry together was magical and she was given the role.

Kate was our captain. She knew about the 12-hour turnaround SAG rules and she was much more savvy as our ringleader. We were very happy to hear what she had to say and we would try to do it. Kate was the one with experience, so if she didn't like a line she would change it. I don't think I knew I could do that at that time.

This photo comes from Farrah herself! It's a picture of her taking a break from filming the episode "The Mexican Connection." (© Farrah Fawcett)

How did you see your character, Jill Munroe?
I saw Jill as being very athletic. I always played a lot of sports, including tennis, horseback riding and skate boarding. So it was just a natural fit. I did a lot of my own stunts. During one I did get hit in the calf by a car. I ran up to it and the car was supposed to drive away real fast. The wheels were turned the wrong way so it spun out when it was driving away and the bumper hit my calf, giving me a huge contusion. Marge, my manger, came to the set and said, 'She can't shoot, look at her leg.' It was dark blue and really swollen. I think I went out and did one more scene, but I was limping. That was the hazardous part of the show! Or being in the middle (between Jaclyn and Kate) handcuffed!

How was it filming "Angels in Chains"?
"Angels in Chains" was fun, and we were like children. It was that show where I think we really bonded, because we were handcuffed together, and we weren't being pulled away to do hair, make-up and all that. So in between scenes we wouldn't even take off the handcuffs. We'd just sit and talk. It was fun. With no pressure of hair, make-up or wardrobe, we could sit outside and watch the crew . . . kind of be a part of the entire process of shooting the scene. That didn't happen very many times. "Angels in Chains" when shown, brought in a 42 share of the audience.

Did you enjoy the Angel frenzy?
Unfortunately, you don't have time to read the letters or the press clips. It just happened so fast that I didn't even realize there were young girls going around pretending to be Jill, Kelly and Sabrina. That was very flattering.

Did you have any problems with stalkers?

In fact, they did have to hire security for me. There was a girl who was on a bus coming to Los Angeles from Louisiana, and she had hundreds of photos of me in a shoe box, along with a gun in there. She told the person sitting next to her that she was my lover and coming out to be with me. And if I didn't want to be with her, that she was going to kill me and then kill herself. When she did not get back on the bus, the woman she was sitting next to called the Los Angeles Police. So for quite a while I had security around me. I never did find out whatever happened to her or that shoebox.

When did it become a closed set?

From the start they pretty much kept the set closed. However, they would bend the rules whenever they had someone special, like John Travolta or Anthony Hopkins, who brought his parents to visit the set. I got to meet Anthony Hopkins and he says "thank you" every time we run into each other.

How was it to come back after you had left?

On my return episodes, I was excited to see the girls. It was fun and shocking how easily we slipped back into our pecking order of which girl said what, and my teasing with Kate and Jaclyn. We had our own little clique, and after all that time had passed, the court and whole big deal, they were happy to see me. Of course, they never wanted me to leave. I actually was so happy the show continued to do well, so I didn't feel guilty about leaving it. Cheryl came in and was instantly likeable and that's to her credit.

How was the photo shoot for the Time *magazine cover?*
Shooting the Time Magazine cover was a great day and one of my fondest memories. I remember walking from the set over to where we were going to shoot the cover, and I looked over at Aaron. I was thinking about all this press we got about being a jiggle show, and here we are shooting the cover for *Time* magazine. So I said "Aaron, not bad . . . the cover of *Time* magazine" and he said, "we're $40,000 over budget on the wardrobe with just this show." I thought, "I don't quite know how to respond." I don't know if he was downplaying it or being a producer saying 'hurry up, hurry up' and don't be feeling too good. We're over budget." We were always over budget with hair, make-up, or wardrobe.

For me, being on the cover of Time magazine was a high point of the show and with it came a certain respect.

Did any funny things happen on the set?
A lot of stuff on the show was adlibbed. Kate was saying the first time she knew it was going to work out well between us was when I was walking out of a scene and she was sitting on the edge of the couch, I just gave Kate a playful shove and she fell into the couch. Totally unrehearsed! The producers loved it and left it in the show. I think it's those magical accidents that made the show seem fresh. That you can't write.

How was it working with David Doyle?
David was wonderful. He lightened everything and was funny. He went with the flow. I don't think I ever heard him complain.

How was it working with your fellow Angels, Kate and Jaclyn?

It was great working with Kate and Jaclyn. It was just a good chemistry mix, and really to this day whenever we see each other, which is often, we go right back into it, sort of giggly, gossipy about what's going on in our lives. I can't imagine the show working without them.

On Cloud Nine with Jaclyn Smith

Certainly the speakerphone was some of the magic of the show. I think it made us imagine this character more so than if we were looking at him. It made it more challenging and I think more intriguing. It was hard at first. Actors connect by the eyes, and here we are doing it to a speaker phone. It was three girls who were really good friends, who were really having fun, and I think it came off that way. I think it added an element of surprise and curiosity. Maybe at the time we wanted him to come in, but it would have been a mistake.

Early on, we had John Forsythe's voice to act to. We demanded in the beginning that he record his voice-over so we could react to it and not somebody reading it. Not every time, but we had that opportunity quite a bit in the first season.—on acting to the speaker box

I remember when auditioning for *Charlie's Angels,* their original idea was to have a blonde, brunette, and a redhead. They had seen me on *Switch* with Eddy Albert and Robert Wagner. So I went in for several readings in Aaron's office and then my final one with Kate and Farrah. They saw something they liked, even though they originally wanted a redhead. So they hired me as the final Angel.

The streetwise angel, Jaclyn Smith, being interviewed during filming of "Angels in Paradise" in 1977. (© Cynthia A. Lai)

Originally the character of Kelly Garrett was written for Kate. I think she wanted to play a part that was more of a departure for her. So she chose to take the role of Sabrina Duncan.

I saw Kelly as a very sensitive, emotional, feeling individual. I saw her really as one for the underdog, because she hadn't had all the opportunities in life. So her heart really went out for that person. She was the most emotional Angel. Whether it was a child or an adult, she wore her heart on her sleeve. She was always looking beyond herself.

The show's success surprised me and did change my life overnight. You're just like a rock star, you're going through backdoors, kitchens, and can no longer stand in line at the movies or at Disneyland.

People reach out to you when you are on television every week. I know I had young girls looking up to me. I connected with some and I corresponded with one little girl who had anorexia. It's a plus when you can give back and connect in a different way. You are touching someone's life. Even with the good, there is bad. I had a lot of restraining orders during that time. One in particular kept trying to break into my home. That was a little scary!

Kate was somewhat of a leader. She would say, "Girls you're not going to forgo your twelve-hour turn around." She was very strong. She had been there before, so she was sort of our leader in the way of what the rules would be. She would say, "We're not going to do this." Farrah and I would say, "OK, Kate," and just went along. We were very compliant. It was all an education to us since it was our first series. I had done *Switch* but it was different, and this was our show.

The series was an education. We had technical advisors show us how to hold a gun. I felt really awkward at first. I think Farrah felt awkward too. Kate had done that on *The Rookies*, so she was ahead of the game. Another one was the karate flip used in the opening titles for me. I was pretty agile and physically fit to handle it, but karate is much different than ballet!

I also liked it when we got to do things that we normally didn't do, such as ice-skating or belly dancing. The undercover stuff was all fun. We all were thirsting for something beyond the Barbie-doll image.

It was difficult when fellow Angels left. I like to go the distance, and it's not easy. Farrah leaving the show was shocking. We were all just devastated. Then Cheryl came in, she was the right choice, and she filled Farrah's shoes. Both are spectacular in their own way, and that is what that character needed. It became sort of part of the game. After Kate left, it just became easier as they brought in a new Angel.

I welcomed Cheryl. I think she is amazing. There were such expectations on her. I admire her because she was up against a lot and she handled it beautifully. Cheryl was a constant professional and she made it fun and gave it her all.

David Doyle was amazing and one of the highpoints of the show. He was funny, and not just his character. He was funny on the set and always in a good mood unless someone stole his Milky Way. He always liked having all his candy bars lined up. He held it all together for us during the turbulence. He was the balance. He would do anything to make us laugh.

When the series ended, I was ready to move on. I was glad I completed my five years, even though at times you think, I want to go do this or that, but I signed a contract. I was grateful for it. Things happen for a reason. It was good for me to do *Charlie's Angels.*

One of my most amazing memories was when Prince Charles came for a visit. How often do you get to meet a prince? Prince Charles was very knowledgeable when he came on the set and was very inquisitive. He wanted to know everything. It was very flattering. I also remember we repainted everything, even the bathrooms! That was pretty outstanding.

If Kate, Farrah, and I would do the show today it would be so different. We were just so young and just starting out. It would be fun to shoot one again today to see how different we would make it.

The original Charlie's Angels, Farrah, Kate, and Jaclyn, during their rehearsal for the tribute to Aaron Spelling on the 2006 Emmy Awards. (© Farrah Fawcett)

CHAPTER TWO

After Angels: Movies, Counterfeits, and Cartoons

SOME WERE sad, some were happy, and some were relieved *Charlie's Angels* had gone to heaven. Kate Jackson, Farrah Fawcett, Jaclyn Smith, Cheryl Ladd, Shelley Hack, and Tanya Roberts all went on to do other work but would always be remembered as being Charlie's Angels.

Kate Jackson went on to do numerous motion pictures, including *Loverboy* and the gay classic, *Making Love.* She once again returned to TV with her mega-hit 1980s TV show, *Scarecrow and Mrs. King,* and later with the TV version of *Baby Boom.* Her career also has opened up the world of directing to her. She became an advocate for the American Heart Association after she found that she had a hole in her heart in the early 1990s, and she is a survivor of breast cancer. In 1995, she adopted her son Taylor, who is her pride and joy. Jackson continues to work in films and television, and in 2007 she made a guest appearance on CBS's *Criminal Minds.*

Farrah Fawcett went on to star on the silver screen in three features after leaving *Charlie's Angels: Somebody Killed Her Husband, Sunburn,* and *Saturn 3.* In the early 1980s, she took a dramatic turn in TV movies, *Murder in Texas, Poor Little Rich Girl,* and *The Burning Bed.* She also worked her acting magic in *Extremities,* both on Broadway and in the theatrical release. When Fawcett turned fifty, she posed nude for *Playboy,* which became the best-selling issue of the 1990s for the company. Two years later, Farrah posed again, but this time she mixed her art with her ageless sexiness. In 2005, she allowed cameras to follow her around in her reality series *Chasing Farrah.*

Jaclyn Smith, the only Angel to stay for all five seasons, went on to become the "Queen of the Miniseries," doing great projects such as *Rage of Angels, George Washington, Florence Nightingale, Windmills of the Gods,* and *Jacqueline Bouvier Kennedy.* In the early 1980s she married director Tony Richmond and had two children, Gaston Anthony and Spencer Margaret. The couple divorced eight years later. In 1985, she teamed up with Kmart to create her own line of clothing. In 1998, she was married, for the fourth time, to Dr. Brad Allen. With her career going full-circle, she stepped back into Kelly Garrett's shoes for a cameo in the 2003 feature film *Charlie's Angels: Full Throttle.* And in 2007, she was the host of Bravo's very successful TV reality show, *Shear Genius.*

Cheryl Ladd went on to do successful projects such as *Now and Forever, Millennium, Poison Ivy, Bluegrass,* and the critically acclaimed *The Grace Kelly Story.* She returned to TV in 1994 with her own series, *One West Waikiki.* In 1996, she and her husband Brian Russell wrote their first children's book, *The Adventures of Little Nettie Windship.* She also costarred with her daughter Jordan Ladd in the Lifetime film, *Every Mother's Worst Fear.* She hit the silver screen again with parts in *Permanent Midnight* and a remake of *A Dog of Flanders.* In 2003, Ladd returned to TV for a third time in the hit NBC series *Las Vegas,* playing the wife of James Caan. And in 2005, she released her second book, *Token Chick: A Woman's Guide to Golfing with the Boys,* talking about her love of golf.

Shelley Hack was rumored for a leading role on *Dallas* after leaving *Charlie's Angels.* The stint never materialized, but she did go on to star in two TV series (*Cutter to Houston* and *Jack and Mike*) several films (*King of Comedy* and *Troll*) and performed off-Broadway. In the 1990s she ran for office in Los Angeles, married Harry Winer, and had a daughter named Rose. Presently, she now is the president of the Shelley Hack Media Consultancy, which specializes in international projects that focus on the intersection between the media and the development of civil society.

Tanya Roberts hung up her halo and crossed over to motion pictures after the series ended. She starred in the cult classics *The Beastmaster* and *Sheena* and then became a Bond girl, Stacey Sutton, in *A View to a Kill.* In October 1981, to cross-promote her first feature, *The Beastmaster,* Roberts was the first Angel to pose nude for *Playboy.* She went on to make several direct-to-video films, *Inner Sanctum, Deep Down,* and *Legal Tender.* In 1998, Roberts returned to primetime TV on

"I have tons of gay friends, and never once have I asked that particular question of them. Which is really interesting. I knew they loved the show; I knew they loved me. But I never asked what it was about the show that they felt so drawn to. I believe it was because it was fun and a little glamorous and we were everyone's best friends, we were such grown-up Girl Scouts. I think everyone thought they would be so fun to hang out with and go on the adventures with us. We were fun girls."

—Cheryl Ladd, on gays loving Charlie's Angels

the hit Fox series *That 70s Show,* playing Midge Pinciotti. Presently she appears in commercials for Tahiti Village.

Emmy Angels

The Angels have reunited a few times since the TV show went off the air in 1981. Kate, Jaclyn, and Cheryl took center stage at the 1992 People's Choice Awards to present a Lifetime Achievement award to Aaron Spelling. In 1994, Farrah, Kate, and Jaclyn showed their pearly whites in a photo shoot for *People* magazine's twentieth anniversary issue, shot by world-famous photographer Herb Ritts. And in 1998, Farrah, Kate, and Jaclyn paid homage to Aaron Spelling in the TV special, *All Star Party for Aaron Spelling.*

In August 2006, Farrah, Kate, and Jaclyn stole the limelight at the fifty-eighth Emmy Awards by making a surprise appearance together. As the stage went black and the *Charlie's Angels* theme music began to play, out they walked. The crowd went wild as they paid tribute to the late Aaron Spelling, who had passed away in June

HEAVENLY TIDBIT

In 2008, Kate Jackson made a guest appearance as a judge on Jaclyn Smith's reality series *Shear Genius.* The twosome assisted in selecting the best updated "*Charlie's Angels* hairdo" by the show's participants/stylists.

2006. The next day, the Angels were the talk of the town. They were showcased in newspapers, magazines, and newscasts. It was like 1976 all over again: the Angels were hot.

Charlie's Angels Minisodes

Charlie's Angels has found a new life online at the Minisode Network, http://myspace.com/minisodenetwork. Episodes have been randomly selected from the first four seasons of the show and edited down to approximately six minutes, including opening credits, basic storyline and plot twists, solving the case, and end credits. What a great way for fans to get a super-quick Angel fix!

Movie Angels

The talk of a *Charlie's Angels* movie had been a rumor in Hollywood for many years. The buzz got a big PR boost in 1998, when many magazines announced that Jada Pinkett-Smith, Michelle Yeoh, and Jenny McCarthy were cast to be Charlie's newest Angels. It was just a tale; those three actresses never joined Charlie's heavenly team.

The rumormongering continued until actress Drew Barrymore took a serious look at the Angels, dusted off their wings, and brought them to the silver screen in 2000. Barrymore's Flower Films teamed up with *Charlie's Angels* TV producer Leonard Goldberg and Sony Pictures. Aaron Spelling's deal with Paramount Pictures at that time excluded him from producing the motion picture. Barrymore cast herself as the first

HEAVENLY TIDBITS

In the cult classic film *Poison Ivy*, Drew Barrymore plays a teenager who has a lesbian affair with her one-and-only friend, Sylvie Cooper (Sara Gilbert). She then proceeds to sleep with Sylvie's father (Tom Skerritt) and eventually pushes Sylvie's mother (Cheryl Ladd) out a window. Not very heavenly!

Angel, and Cameron Diaz was cast as the second Angel, but the search for the third Angel took a while. Actress Thandie Newton was announced as the new Angel but then declined in order to costar with Tom Cruise in *Mission Impossible 2*. The producers continued their search, and a very short time later, Lucy Liu took on the role of the third Angel.

In 2000, *Charlie's Angels* was introduced to a whole new audience. It was as if Charles Townsend Private Investigations had never closed its doors. Charlie's latest Angels were Dylan Sanders (Barrymore), Natalie Cook (Diaz), and Alex Mundy (Liu). The agency was still run by good-old-dependable Bosley (Bill Murray), and the office had a similar, yet updated look to it.

The original script was written by Ryan Rowe and Ed Solomon. The story line had the Angels infiltrating and eliminating a band of robotic female models who were trying to take over the world.

Then John August, an up-and-coming Hollywood writer who had made a name for himself with the hit film *Go,* was brought in to revise the script. August went back to the show's original roots, keeping with the simplicity and the heart of the series, but also bringing the Angels into the new millennium.

In this new script, the Angels are hired to stop an evil programmer from releasing everyone's private information. As it all unfolds, they find that it was actually a ploy by the client to track down and kill Charlie. But thanks to their brains, wits, sex appeal, and some very cool toys worthy of James Bond, the Angels save Charlie's life once again!

The Angels of the new millennium have some similarities with the classic Angels. Here are a just a few of their crossover traits:

Dylan Sanders (Drew Barrymore) is reminiscent of Sabrina Duncan (Kate Jackson). Sanders is the team leader who brings her fellow Angels together and gets them going on the case. She is also streetwise and in-your-face like Julie Rogers (Tanya Roberts).

Natalie Cook (Cameron Diaz) has the blonde characteristics of both Jill and Kris Munroe. She has smooth dancing moves, is very athletic, and knows how to skateboard.

Alexandra "Alex" Munday (Lucy Liu) combines the talents of Kelly Garrett (Jaclyn Smith) with Tiffany Welles (Shelley Hack). She is an electronics expert who can pick locks while karate-chopping men twice her size. And she has a high sense of fashion.

Kate Jackson, Farrah Fawcett, and Jaclyn Smith were asked to be in the film. It was rumored that they each requested a million dollars for their appearance. Fawcett felt it would be fun if she played Charlie, but that idea was turned down. Both Cheryl Ladd and Tanya Roberts expressed interest in the movie, but neither was approached. Ultimately, none of them were in the film.

Charlie's Angels hit theaters on November 3, 2000, and brought in $264 million worldwide.

A Gay Old Time!

- The meeting between Bosley and Roger Corwin turns hot and bothered with some very gay overtones. Bosley gay? Come on, Boz, take one for the team!
- Dylan and Natalie dive head first into cross-dressing, all the way down to facial hair and using the urinal in the men's restroom.

Charlie's Angels: Full Throttle

After the huge success of the *Charlie's Angels* movie, the Angels return to the office for another case. This time they are hired to retrieve the H.A.L.O. (Hidden Alias List Operations) rings, which hold all the names of the people in the FBI's witness protection program. The Angels have to go up against former-Angel-gone-bad Madison Lee (Demi Moore) who is trying to kill the Angels and sell off the H.A.L.O. rings.

Barrymore, Diaz, and Liu all returned for the second film. The only major cast change was the replacement of Bosley. Comedian Bernie Mac took over the

HEAVENLY TIDBITS

This sequel was originally titled *Charlie's Angels: H. A.L.O.* but was changed in production to the edgier *Charlie's Angels: Full Throttle.* If you watch closely when Madison is in the Townsend office, you can see the infamous Hall of Angels, featuring the photos of Angels past and present. If you look even closer, you can make out Julie Rogers (Tanya Roberts). A sequence was shot of the Hall of Angels but was never used in the film.

role played by Bill Murray. The highlight was the return of original Angel Kelly Garrett (Jaclyn Smith). In a dream-like sequence, Kelly shares her Angelic wisdom with Dylan. Scriptwriter John August wrote the scene to be a "Yoda" moment for Dylan, who was about to leave the agency.

Charlie's Angels: Full Throttle pulled in $259 million and hit theaters on June 27, 2003.

A Gay Old Time!

- Disguised as the C.S.I. team leader, Natalie shows her very masculine/dyke side.
- When Natalie meets Madison on the beach, the two have a very strong lesbian/sexual tension that almost results in a kiss. Now that is something for Bosley to put into the next *Angelic Heaven* newsletter.

Charlie's Angels: Animated Adventures

The Angels turned into full-blown animation for this online series. Serving as a prequel to *Charlie's Angels: Full Throttle,* the series had six episodes, each approximately two to three minutes long. The Angels are working on case number 062703: The Kidnapping. U.S. Marshall Ray Carter has gone missing after being lured to an all-male club. This series takes the viewer up to where the movie opens, with the Angels trying rescue Ray Carter from a Russian bar.

Throughout the animated adventure, the Angels don't speak at all except for the opening "Good morning, Charlie." The other odd thing about the series is that the Angels do not resemble Barrymore, Diaz, or Liu—except for hair color. Watch them online at www.animatedangels.com

Counterfeit Angels!

Angels '88 *(1988–1989)*

Aaron Spelling partnered up with the new Fox network channel to create a new TV series, *Angels '88.* The premise had a twist; the four Angels are former actresses who start their own detective agency after their TV detective series had been cancelled. The actresses cast were Claire Yarlett as Connie Bates, Karen Kopins as Pam Ryan,

Sandra Canning as Trisha Lawrence, and Téa Leoni as Bernie Colter. Leoni was the only Angel cast outside Los Angeles during their eleven-city casting tour.

The series had many mishaps getting on the air, including script issues. With time pushing on, the title changed from *Angels '88* into *Angels '89.* Then due to a writers strike, the series was dissolved before a pilot episode had been shot. With the cancellation, Aaron Spelling Productions was given the green light on a replacement show, *Beverly Hills 90210.* The show ran for ten seasons and produced the equally successful spin-off series, *Melrose Place,* which ran for seven seasons.

Angeles *(1999)*

In 1999, Sony Entertainment bought the Spanish network Telemundo. The studio dipped into its classic

HEAVENLY TIDBITS

Actress Téa Leoni was discovered during the *Angels '88* talent search. She was selected after she wrote "YIKES!" on her headshot. It grabbed the attention of the casting people. Leoni went on to star in the 1995 TV series *The Naked Truth,* which ran for three seasons. She also moved into features, including *Jurassic Park III, Deep Impact, Spanglish,* and, most recently, *Fun with Dick and Jane.* Leoni married David Duchovny of *The X Files* fame and has two children.

library to update old TV shows, including a new Spanish version of *Charlie's Angels* called *Angeles*. This time around, the three Angels have checkered pasts and are hired by the mysterious and reclusive Charlie to fight crime as private eyes. The Angels are Patricia Manterola as Adriana Vega, Sandra Vidal as Elena Sanchez, and Magali Caicedo as Gina Navarro. They are strong women with special talents and hidden resources; they are forced to become a team, relying on their wits and each other, to survive their deadly adventures. Their only contact with Charlie is through David Bose, played by Mauricio Mendoza. The Angeles Investigaciones was located in the coastal town of Costa Rosa.

Storylines from the original TV series were updated, including "Night of the Strangler" and "Angels in Chains." After thirteen episodes, the Angeles headed off to heaven once again.

Asian Charlie's Angels (2001)

Around the world, *Asian Charlie's Angels* made its premiere. Filmed in Mandarin, this Taiwanese version featured Kelly Lin as Cindy, Ying Qu as Betty, and Annie Wu as Annabelle. The three Angels had it all: martial arts prowess, technical skills, and sex appeal. It is unknown how many shows were shot. The first episode had the Angels tracking down a serial killer who targeted young, wealthy socialites.

Behind the Camera: The Unauthorized Story of Charlie's Angels *(2004)*

A very "loosely" based TV adaptation purporting to reveal how the TV series came about. It follows the trials and tribulations of Farrah Fawcett, Jaclyn Smith, and Kate Jackson up until the beginning of season two of the series, when Cheryl Ladd joined the cast. Tricia Helfer portrayed Farrah Fawcett, Lauren Stamile was Kate Jackson, Christina Chambers was Jaclyn Smith, and Chelsea Watson was Cheryl Ladd.

The film did get some fanfare but was not well received by the original stars of the show. Jay Bernstein, Farrah Fawcett's 1970s manager, was brought on board as an "unofficial" consultant. Bernstein later threatened to sue NBC if they did not delete the final scene of him walking down Hollywood Boulevard looking for his newest "Farrah" look-alike, which he said it was a defamation of character and would hurt his business. The scene was edited out of the original TV airing but was included when the show re-aired on Lifetime TV and in the official DVD release.

Wilde Engel *(2002, 2003, 2005)*

This version was created for the German viewing audience. The original pilot aired in 2002 and became a series in 2003. The Angels cast were Birgit Stauber as Christina Rabe, Susann Uplegger as Franziska Borgardt, and Eva Habermann as Lena Heitmann. They're full of girl power, with special talents in technology and combat. Together, they are an unbeatable team against crime. After the first season ended with eight episodes, all three Angels were replaced. Cast were Vanessa Petruo as Rebecca, Tanja Wenzel as Ida, and Zora Holt as Aiko. The second season (2005) lasted only four episodes before their wings were clipped.

Carlito's Angels *(2003)*

It's *Charlie's Angels* set in the New York hood. The Angels—Roxy (Evly Pacheco), Tina (Alessandra Ramos), and Marisol (Jeni Garcia)—received their assignments from their boss Carlito, who is calling from his prison phone. These three Angels fight deadbeat dads and low-life thugs to finding missing welfare checks. No matter if they are broke or unemployed, these three ultra-hot Angels are always on the case.

Hello Darling *(2008)*

This latest version of *Charlie's Angels,* from India, turns the efforts of the crime-fighting trio into a comedy. Produced by Subhash Ghaim and directed by Manoj Tiwari, it stars Gul Panag, Isha Koppikar, and Celina Jaitley as the Angels.

Angel Effects on TV

Even today, the Angels still continue to make ripples in television. They are constantly being emulated when they're not being parodied. Being an Angel has never been so heavenly!

Benny Hill Down Under, *"Archie's Angels" (April 12, 1978), and* Benny Hill, *"Charlene's Angels" (February 6, 1980)*

Benny Hill loved to make fun of TV shows. He spoofed the series on two occasions, the first time around with "Archie's Angels." Benny in full drag took on the role of Jill Munroe. Jill wasn't the smart one of the bunch, but at least she had the help of Kelly and Sabrina (also played by men in drag) to help solve the case. His second rendition featured role reversal with "Charlene's Angels." This time around three men worked for a woman named Charlene. Poor fellows, they always had girls coming on to them while they were solving a case. What hardships!

Saturday Night Live *(February 24, 1979)*

With Kate Jackson as the guest host, you just knew something humorous was brewing. The opening skit had Charlie giving instructions to the Angels, They were to infiltrate the NBC network and assist in sabotaging their TV programming. This time around, Jackson played Sabrina, with Jane Curtain as Kris (Cheryl), Gilda Radner as Kelly (Jaclyn), and John Belushi as Bosley (David).

Baywatch, *"Baywatch Angels" (February 12, 1996)*

Baywatch made a big splash with viewers and gave jiggle TV a new home. This hysterical episode had the *Baywatch* babes dream what would they do if they were Charlie's Angels. The *Baywatch* "Angels" arrive undercover as lifeguards, and get themselves into many perils. Defusing a bomb on an exercise machine and getting kidnapped were never so much fun. Pamela Anderson takes on the character of Jill Munroe, with Yasmine Bleeth as Kelly Garrett and Alexandra Paul as Sabrina Duncan.

Married with Children, *"The Hood, the Bud, and the Kelly" (January 7, 1996)*

In order to film an exercise video for Kelly (Christina Applegate), Bud (David Faustino) borrows money from the mob. However, his life is threatened when Kelly refuses to finish the video after having a disagreement with the male lead. If a compromise isn't made soon, Bud won't live out rest of the day. Luckily, three of his backup dancers, Farrah, Jaclyn, and Kate, turn out to be undercover cops. The Angels were played by: Lisa Arturo as Farrah, Veronica De La Cruz as Kate and Melissa De Sousa as Jaclyn

V.I.P. *(1998–2002)*

While at a movie premiere, hot dog stand employee Vallery Irons (Pamela Anderson) inadvertently saves celebrity Brad Cliff from getting killed by a psychotic fan. After being mistaken for being a bodyguard, she is approached by Tasha Dexter (Molly Culver) and Nikki Franco (Natalie Raitano) to be the "face" for their new up-and-coming bodyguard agency. With Anderson in the lead, crime doesn't stand a chance!

Charmed *(1998–2006)*

A show about the supernatural Halliwell sisters, Prue (Shannen Doherty), Piper (Holly Marie Combs), and Phoebe (Alyssa Milano), who reunite after the passing of their grandmother. Unbeknownst to them, they are the "Charmed Ones" and immediately go up against demons and dark forces while finding out they are witches. After Prue dies in a tragic mishap, half-sister Paige

HEAVENLY NOTE

The replacement of Doherty with McGowan mimicked Farrah Fawcett's replacement with Cheryl Ladd on *Charlie's Angels:* a rookie who makes mistakes but always lands on her feet. And in 2005, Cheryl Ladd guest-starred as the Charmed Ones' new stepmother. Then they find out she was a demon who married their father in order to get close enough to Wyatt, Piper's son, to kidnap him.

Matthews (Rose McGowan) steps forward to continue the fight of good versus evil.

Celebrity DeathMatch, *"The Prisoners" (October 8, 2000)*

In this ring we have battling Angels—Farrah Fawcett versus Drew Barrymore—fighting their way to the top. Making this claymationfest even more fun is Charlie talking to the dueling Angels over a speakerphone.

She Spies *(2002–2004)*

Combine *Charlie's Angels* with *V.I.P.* and you have *She Spies*. Cassie (Natasha Henstridge), DD (Kristen Miller), and Shane (Natashia Williams) form a threesome plucked from prison by a clandestine government organization and given a choice: either to spend their best years under lock and key or to enlist with the good guys, putting their considerable criminal talents to more patriotic use. Working for the Feds that put them away, the career con-girls have turned their backs on their former lives, waging war on the lowliest of the world's sleaze and scumbags. Armed with sleek moves, street smarts, and enough attitude to make a sailor blush, these "bad-girls-turned-good" make the Navy Seals look like the Coast Guard, and make the Coast Guard look like the Girl Scouts.

D.E.B.S. *(2004)*

Amy (Sara Foster), Max (Meagan Good), Janet (Jill Ritchie), and Dominique (Devin Aoki) are known as D.E.B.S., a group of college students who are undercover spies for the U.S. government and fight international criminals while never having a hair out of place or their makeup smudged. As D.E.B.S. leader Amy goes up against dyke bad girl Lucy Diamond (Jordana Brewster), a lesbian love match is formed, pitting Amy against the other D.E.B.S.

That '70s Show, *"Kiss of Death" (March 20, 2000)*

After being rushed into surgery and put under anesthesia, Fez (Wilmer Valderrama) calls out for Charlie's Angels. As he goes under, he dreams about "Fez's Angels," a trio of lovelies (Laura Prepon, Mila Kunis, and Lisa Robin Kelly) who risk their lives to save their infamous unseen boss Fez.

HEAVENLY NOTE

Angel Tanya Roberts costarred on *That '70s show*, playing Midge Pinciotti, the mother of lead character Donna. And if you look closely while watching the series, you will see Farrah Fawcett's iconic swimsuit poster hanging on the wall of Eric Foreman's bedroom.

Fat Actress, *"Charlie's Angels" (March 14, 2005)*

In this scripted reality series, Kirstie Alley does everything in her power to land a prime role in the upcoming movie *Charlie's Angels III*. The Angels have very interesting characteristics this time around: one is a little person, one is extra-tall, and the other is overweight. What has Charlie gotten himself into?

So Notorious *(2006)*

In this reality-based series based on the true-life adventures of Tori Spelling, there are *Charlie's Angels* references in every episode, from her father (Aaron Spelling) talking to her only via speakerphone to flashbacks of Tori on

HEAVENLY NOTE

Farrah was Tori Spelling's real-life next-door neighbor. The bit in the first episode of *So Notorious* about Farrah needing a potato is a true story!

HEAVENLY NOTE

The "Lady of the Lake" parody was written by Molly Fisher, an *L Word* contest winner.

the set of *Charlie's Angels* and having Farrah Fawcett as her next-door neighbor. What a tribute to the Angels!

The L Word, *"Lady of the Lake" (January 22, 2008)*

Once upon a time there were three little lesbians . . . and now they work for me, and my name is Bev. In this hilarious spoof, the Angels: Kelly (Rachel Shelley), Sabrina (Kate Moennig), and Jill (Leisha Hailey), with the help of Bosley (Laurel Holloman), go undercover to find out if their new friend Jenny is lesbian, bisexual, or straight using their gaydar guns.

Cartoon Angels

Captain Caveman and the Teen Angels *(1977–1980)*

This is the story of the Teen Angels, Brenda (the Kelly Garrett of the group, with brown hair), Taffy (modeled after Jill Munroe, all the way down to the big blonde hair), and DeeDee (the African-American version of Sabrina Duncan), who free stone-age superhero Captain

Caveman from a block of ice while searching a cave. Captain Caveman becomes their constant companion, lives above the Teen Angels van, and assists them in solving all their cases.

Alvin and the Chipmunks, *"Alvie's Angels"—August 29, 2000*

Alvin sends his crime-fighting trio of Angels, the Chipettes, out on their latest case to track down a jewel thief Chad Fleming.

The Powerpuff Girls *(1998–2004)*

Once upon a time, there were three little kindergarten girls. Blossom is a redhead and the leader of the group, Buttercup is a brunette and a tomboy, and Bubbles is a blonde and the sweetest member of the group. They were created by Professor Utoni, who made them out of sugar, spice, and everything nice, but Chemical X was also added, which gave the girls superpowers. Now between kindergarten and playtime, the Powerpuff Girls save the town of Townsville from evil villains.

South Park, *"Two Guys Naked in a Hot Tub" (July 21, 1999)*

When attending a meteor party with his parents at Mr. Mackey's house, Stan gets stuck in the basement with Pip, Dougie, and Butters. They each take on one of the Angels' personalities after finding a trunk full of women's clothing. Butters plays Kelly Garrett, Dougie plays Jill Munroe, and Pip plays Sabrina Duncan, with Stan giving the Angels their mission.

Totally Spies! *(2001)*

Three Beverly Hills High School girls, Sam, Alex, and Clover, are secret agents who fight international criminals for their boss Jerry James Lewis, the head of the World Organization of Human Protection (WOOHP). Sam has long, flowing red hair and is the smart one; Clover has medium-length blonde hair and is the most cynical; and Alex with short black hair is very athletic and a bit clumsy. The girls have to balance their high school issues with saving the world on a daily basis, not to mention handling their school rival, Mandy.

Chico's Angels

In the 1990s came the very successful stage production of *The Brady Bunch,* and it made theatergoers laugh at their All-American favorite family. So how could a stage production of *Charlie's Angels* be far behind? Enter Oscar Quintero and his Latino "drag" Angels, who created a cult classic theater experience with *Chico's Angels.*

I used to do a show called *The Plush Life,* which is a drag improv soap opera. We did a night where one of the characters was having legal problems, so she needed to hire a detective to find out who was harassing her. So we decided to do *Charlie's Angels,* from the start we were the three Angels; we did the whole *Destiny's Child* song. We did a parody of the song into the actual opening "Good Morning, Charlie" type thing and I played Kelly Garrett, of course. It evolved and each time we came out, we were a different Angel. Jill Munroe leaves

Angels? Nope, these heavenly beauties are Chico's Angels.
Oh, Charlie! (© Gina Ortiz)

and in comes Kris Munroe, and the next scene Tiffany comes in and Sabrina was out, and the last scene Julie came in. It was the funniest thing how every time the Angels kept changing. But that night ended up being such a blast onstage that I got the idea I wanted to make a Latino version and I remembered the Spanish TV series *Angeles.* That idea set the whole thing in motion.

One of my favorite episodes of *Charlie's Angels* was "Pretty Angels All in a Row." Plus I love beauty pageants. So I thought, Why not combine my two favorite things? So I started writing a version of "Pretty Angels all in a Row," and I called it "Pretty Chicos All in a Row." It was like, "These three Latin girls who went to the Police Academy all failed and all were from different parts of Latin America: one was from East L.A., one was from Mexico, and one was from Cuba."

Chico's Angels was the best thing that ever happened to me, because it became this little weird cult hit that summer of 2003. We ended up writing and performing a second episode and then a third episode and we've been doing it for four years now. Now we've just completed our first trailer for MySpace TV. Wherever *Chico's Angels* ends up, whether it's on TV, Broadway, or elsewhere, I always want to do the stage show. It's the most fun I have ever had. People love it; they get that we are celebrating the Latino quirks.

I think that *Charlie's Angels* appeals to gay men because gay men seem to like things which are a little off-kilter. Things that don't fit into a mold just like we don't. I think that is why it's so easy to relate to the Angels because they are going against society's ideas of what a woman should be and against the idea of what a man

CELEBRITY SURVEY #2: WHEN AND WITH WHOM DID YOU FIRST WATCH *CHARLIE'S ANGELS*?

"I watched summer repeats with my brother and mom, all through the 1970s."

—John August, screenwriter, *Charlie's Angels, Charlie's Angels: Full Throttle, Go*

"Surreptitiously, alone, with the volume down low, so I didn't have to explain the fascination to my feminist mother."

—Peter Paige, actor, *Queer as Folk*

"The night the series premiered with my Mom and my Dad. My Dad hated it. He said, 'There is no way chicks can fight crime.' I ran to the back of the house and turned into Wonder Woman in that very second because I sensed danger."

—ANT, comedian, actor, *Last Comic Standing*

"With my sister Jaan, as soon as it debuted. There weren't a ton of things to do in Chattanooga, Tennessee, and the debut got tons of hype."

—Lady Bunny, Ladybunny.net

"I honestly don't remember the first time I watched, but it was my favorite show. My mom would punish me by not letting me watch, and it would just kill me. You don't think I was born a lesbian, do you?"

—Michelle Wolff, actress, *Dante's Cove*

"I watched it alone in my bedroom in Scottsdale, Arizona. If I was watching with anyone else, I couldn't have done the dialogue and flipped the towel on my head that was serving as a makeshift Farrah wig."

—Jackie Beat, Jackiebeatrules.com

"I watched the show in repeats. That is when I remember the show, but I also remember watching it as a little kid. I remember my sisters would watch it, and that is the only night they would let me stay up late because it used to be on at 10 o'clock. One time I got in terrible trouble, and they made me go to bed early. I threw a fit because they were not going to let me watch *Charlie's Angels,* and I'm not going to be able to fall asleep until *Charlie's Angels* is over. I sat there and cried. Because *Charlie's Angels* was happening without me."

—Oscar Quintero, creator of *Chico's Angels*

"I was really young. I believe I watched it with my mother and father. But I was addicted from the second it was on. Women in peril, love it!"

—Chi Chi LaRue, porn director

"I wasn't allowed to stay up late enough to watch the first season of *Charlie's Angels* because it aired at 10 p.m. By the second season, my sister and I were glued to the season premiere of "Angels in Paradise" at 9 p.m. Bikini Kris . . . WOWZA!"

—Glen Hanson, artist glenhanson.com

"My parents and I got behind 'Jiggle TV' from the get-go. I can actually say that *Charlie's Angels* brought my father and me closer together. It was the one TV show that he *didn't* sleep through. He had no idea that I was watching the show just for the hair.

—Frank DeCaro, host, *The Frank DeCaro Show* on Sirius

"I tried to watch it with my brothers, who were too young to be mesmerized by the girls, but I usually watched it with best friend, my neighbor Johnny, who was my age and turned out to be gay. Which was not a surprise."

—Julie Brown, comedian, actress, and singer

"The first time I watched *Charlie's Angels* was with my best friend. I was twelve and watching it on Nick-at-Nite. I was like, 'This is fricken' brilliant television,' it was so funny. The Angels were a nightmare, the acting was misery, and the script was beyond comprehension, but I loved it, this is an amazing piece of work. From then on my love of the Angels continued to blossom."

—Dylan Vox, actor, *The Lair*

should be like. Gay men fit into that box, and so do Charlie's Angels. I think that is why gay men love the Angels. They were fabulous, and what gay man does not like a fabulous woman?

On Cloud Nine Q&A with Leonard Goldberg

Q: *In recreating the film versions of your TV show, what was the main concern for you?*

A: The main concern was that we wanted to create a movie that was not just another episode of the TV show, and we also tried to keep in mind that certain images and values had changed in our society, particularly in the way that women were represented since we first did the show.

Author Mike Pingel with *Charlie's Angels* producer Leonard Goldberg at the premiere of *Charlie's Angels* the movie in 2000. (© Mike Pingel)

Q: *Finding the right Angels for the feature film—was that a hard task to match the stable of Angels you already established?*
A: Yes, it was extremely hard because we didn't just want to say . . . she's going to be Jackie Smith, she's going to be Kate Jackson, and she's going to be Farrah. We didn't want to put together a road company of the original Angels; we wanted the new Angels to be distinct, in and of themselves.

Q: *While making the films, how important was keeping in touch with the original feeling of the series?*
A: The image of women in our society had changed so much, but I did want to make the Angels positive role models for young girls and women.

Q: *What was your favorite part from the feature films?*
A: What I like most about the films was the dancing (which we never had in the series) and the level to which we took the Angels' action sequences.

Q: *In the feature film, what was with the decision not have the Angels carry guns like they did in the TV series?*
A: We had a strong feeling that there was so much violence in our country that if the Angels could accomplish their missions without the use of guns, it would be a positive statement.

Q: *When you created the idea of* The Alley Cats, *did you ever think that you were creating a group of real-life superheroes who would still, thirty-plus years later, have such an effect on the world?*

A: No. As I said at our premiere in London, if anyone had suggested to me when we first started the *Charlie's Angels* series that thirty years later I would be standing on a pink carpet at the London premiere of a *Charlie's Angels* movie, I would have asked them what they were smoking and could they pass it over.

On Cloud Nine with Cheryl Ladd

It was very odd acting to the speaker phone, but I got used to it. The fun thing with the actual show was hearing Forsythe's great voice, because on the set a script girl read his lines.

As a young actress in Hollywood, I was working hard to perfect my craft, and I enrolled in the best acting classes in town. My very first professional jobs were *Josie and the Pussycats* and the comedy/variety hour, *The Ken Berry "Wow" Show.* Small guest-staring roles in *The Rookies, Ironside,* and *The Streets of San Francisco* followed, and I found myself playing the All-American girl who was killed in the first minutes of the show.

Surprisingly, those small parts were getting me noticed. I was offered bigger and better roles on popular series like *Happy Days, Police Story,* and *Fantastic Journey.* Then I found myself auditioning for Spelling and Goldberg's new show *Family,* for the role of Nancy Lawrence. I felt the writing was topnotch, and I really wanted to be part of a quality show. I thought it was a good role for me. I did come very close to being cast, but as luck would have it, the part was given to Meredith Baxter-Birney.

Then all the hoopla began with the news that Farrah Fawcett was leaving *Charlie's Angels.* It was a huge buzz around Hollywood. The search for Charlie's Newest

Angel was on, and I was asked to audition for the role. Aaron Spelling felt I would be perfect as the new Angel and offered me the part twice, which I turned down. My friends in acting class thought I was crazy for passing on the role. As fate would have it, my ex-husband David Ladd and I were out to dinner, and Aaron came over to our table and convinced me to at least come in for a meeting. He was so sweet, so of course I agreed.

At the meeting, I let him know I really didn't see myself playing such a glamorous character, and, let's face it, they were some big shoes to fill. I suggested that I wanted to be more comedic, and Aaron said, "Why couldn't you be?" He and I created the character of Kris Munroe together. Aaron suggested that the character should be Jill's (Farrah's character's) little sister. The role sounded fun and challenging, so I accepted the part.

The powers at ABC decided to have me film my first episode as my screen test. The first episode I shot was "Circus of Terror," and it remains one of my favorites. When Aaron and Len saw the footage, it was done. I was the new Angel.

We all flew to Hawaii to film the opening episode, "Angels in Paradise," and the media frenzy began. I had not changed at all, but overnight I was the most interesting person in the world. I was exactly the same girl I was the week before I became the new Angel, but now everyone was fascinated about my diet, my fashion sense, and my every opinion on everything. I think I kept my bearings because I never forgot I was Cheryl Jean Stoppelmoor from Huron, South Dakota.

Replacing Farrah was daunting. She was such a huge

Cheryl Ladd takes a break from filming "Angel Hunt" in season four. (©catrescue@monmouth.com/Nancy Barr-Brandon)

phenomenon, and I felt the weight of the entire series on my shoulders. What if I failed? What if no one liked me? I liked playing Kris; she was fun, and I hoped if I was having fun, everyone else watching would too.

After the dust settled and the ratings came in for the opening episode, the show continued to bring in the big Nielsen numbers. I was relieved, as were my fellow cast members, the crew, and the producers.

I think Charlie's Angels were truly just grownup Girl Scouts. We never cussed, fooled around, or were mean to anyone. We were the All-American Girls who fought crime with our wits and brains and sometimes with our bikinis! Eventually, when the ratings would dip, I found myself yet again in another bikini.

Charlie's Angels changed my life in so many ways. I'm proud of my work as an Angel. I enjoy hearing from women fans how much the show changed their lives. We definitely became role models.

When I look back at *Charlie's Angels,* I will always remember the raspy laughter of the very sweet David Doyle. He was such an anchor for me during my four years on the series. I still remember my first day on the set, when David said, "Come on, girl, you're going to be great." I also thank my great pal and fellow Angel, Jaclyn Smith. Without her, I don't think I could have made it.

The athletic angel, Farrah Fawcett, having her hair done in between shots on "Angel Trap" in 1977. (©catrescue@monmouth.com/Nancy Barr-Brandon)

CHAPTER THREE

Heavenly Hair with José Eber

JOSE EBER is the man with a golden hairdryer. He has made some of the most beautiful women of Hollywood even more beautiful, and he helped create the "Farrah hairdo." He has some tips to get you that heavenly look.

My biggest tip, darling, to get "Angel" hair is large rollers! That is extremely important, especially during those times of *Charlie's Angels* and the 1970s. But even today, using very large-sized rollers in order to lift the roots is extremely important. Then you take the hair blower and put a little heat on the rollers and let them cool off. You take them out, flip your head upside-down, and shake your hair with your fingers. Next, take a little hairspray, and spray your hair upside down. Then throw your hair back, and there you go—you're an Angel! That's a very famous trick of mine that I have been using for thirty years.

The most important way to achieve those different "Angel" looks is the cut. Farrah's hair was not one length; it was layered, layered, and layered. Not short layers but layers everywhere. If you wanted to have Farrah's hair, the cut was very important. Totally frame the face with layering, some long wispy bangs, and long layers in the back. Farrah had some enormous, amazing hair. Big rollers are very important.

Jaclyn's hair was not as layered as Farrah's; it was much more one length with some very long invisible layering in order to get that look. To make sure her hair is not super-flat on top, use Velcro rollers to lift the hair and then use some smaller rollers in the bottom part to get some curls.

With Kate Jackson, her base is a blunt cut. She did not want it to be curly. To achieve that sort of look, you blow it dry. And in order to get roots lifted, use big rollers again!

Cheryl Ladd had that fresh, "All American," pretty girl hair. Contrary to Farrah's layered hair, Cheryl's was more one length. In order to get the "Kris" bouncy curls, her hair would be set with big rollers. Afterwards it would be parted down the middle and pulled back on the sides to get that "girl next door" look. It gave a totally fresh look to the new Angel.

Jill. Kelly.

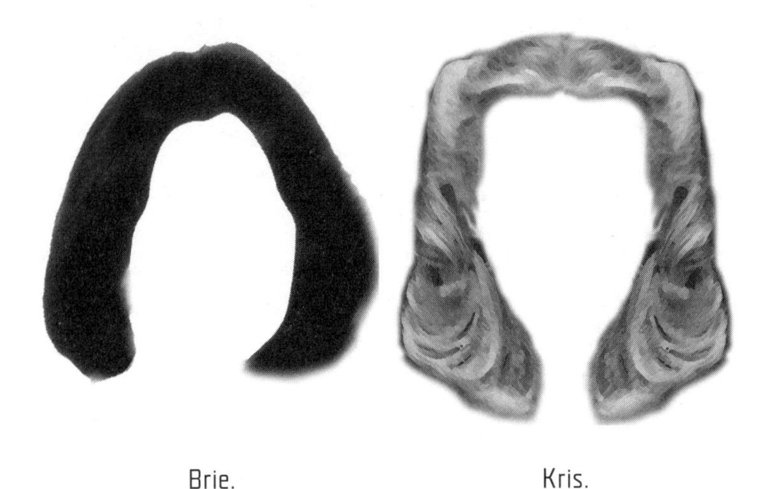

Brie. Kris.

"It got really tiring. I use to have nightmares about hair brushes marching towards me. Cans of hairspray attacking me. By the end of four years, my hair was pretty thrashed. My hair was ready for a rest also!"

—Cheryl Ladd

Angel Hair Wrap Up

You need to create a base for your *Charlie's Angels* hair. Blow it dry, put it in your *large* rollers, make sure to lift the roots, and you don't have to go under the dryer. Just put a little heat on the roller, and let them sit while you're applying makeup or trying on your clothes. When you're done, take out the rollers. If it's not curly enough, brush that area, then take your curling iron and in certain sections, just curl it more. Darling, you'll look like an *Angel*!

Angel Hair No-No

Many believe that when you use a curling iron, you can achieve any of the Angels' styles. Curling irons just will not work. It'll either make your roots flat or your hair too curly.

The Little Detectives

Don't you wish you were able to run around with Charlie's Angels as a kid? Well Cynthia A. Lai from Hawaii did just that! When the Angels arrived in Hawaii back in 1977, she was just fifteen years old. With her brother and cousin, they set out on an Angel adventure which should be called "Angels in Paradise Exposed"! The pint-size trio of Hawaiian detectives got their first look at Charlie's newest Angel, Cheryl Ladd. And Cynthia

"I remember one afternoon Barney Rosenzweig asked why my hair was so flat on the top. I told him I had played tennis at lunch. He wanted my hair reset. I told him that it would take about an hour and I really didn't want production to be held up. He said, 'We'll wait.' As my hair was being restyled, everyone on set waited, and then we went on filming. So yes, my Angel hair had become important, and contrary to rumors I often tried to minimize the hair so we could focus on the scenes and keep the overtime down."

—Farrah Fawcett

José Eber's big hair tip had to do with big rollers as the key to Angel hair. Here is Shelley Hack demonstrating how she got her Angel hair. (©catrescue@monmouth.com/Nancy Barr-Brandon)

snapped some great photos of her favorite Angel, Kate Jackson.

"Security was minimal back then. They only roped off areas when filming. Other than that, you were able to get up close to their trailers, and catch them as they walked by.

"Locals used to take time off from work to watch them film. I remember one teenager that came to Hawaii from the mainland by himself to hang out at the hotel everyday. I also met photographer Ron Galella and other paparazzi that hung out at the hotel everyday.

"After they left, we were able to go through their hotel rooms and rummage around for stuff they left behind.

"I believe it's the strong women thing. I think gay men love strong women. These strong women can take care of themselves, get out of situations and predicaments by using their feminine wiles or bravado. It works. It's the chick factor. Gay men love tough chicks!"

—Chi Chi LaRue

The oddest thing we did was look on the floor for their hair. We have all the Angels' hair! Weird, but they were famous for the hair, right?"

Cynthia still has her Angel hair, and her memory of meeting the Angels is still so vivid. Check out some of her personal photos throughout the book!

On Cloud Nine Q&A with José Eber

Q: *Do you have your favorite Angel hair?*

A: My favorite during those days, obviously I would say Farrah for personal reasons. Farrah was my first celebrity client, and I feel she was very much responsible for giving me a huge break. I always said it even when she denies it.

On top of that, Farrah had the most amazing hair, ideal for a hairdresser because it has a natural wave and there's a lot of it. And it has a mind of its own, but it's a great mind. Obviously it looked better on her than on everyone else who ever tried it and never looked as great. Farrah was very talented with her own hair. I have said it over and over: everyone wanted to take credit for Farrah's hair. The person to be credited for Farrah's hair is Farrah's hair. All the credit should go to Farrah.

Q: *Whose Angel's style was requested the most in the 1970s?*

A: Darling, this is not even a question. You know the answer: it was Farrah. Everybody and their brother wanted to look like Farrah and have Farrah's hair. There were some awful imitations, as you know.

What people didn't realize is that you need a very certain texture of hair to get that look. All the girls with baby-fine hair that was straight as a stick; it didn't work for them. They were using a curling iron and sometimes it just looked atrocious, but some of them did manage. This was the most requested style around the world, not just America. I mean everybody wanted that look.

Q: *What do you think of Angel hair?*
A: To me Angel hair was sexy. Any time you can shake your hair—it's sexy. Touchable hair is sexy hair. I'm a big fan of Angel hair? You bet!

Q: *Do you think the Angel looks hold up?*
A: The Angel styles still work today. But like fashion, it just adapted. Look at Farrah's hair; everybody had it from Heidi Klum, Beyoncé, Halle Berry, and now Madonna with an updated interpretation. In the 1970s it was puffier, fuller, and bigger; now it's less puffy. All those looks in that decade are today much smaller in scale.

Q: *Did you have a crush on one of the Angels?*
A: Farrah. Funny, I use to wear my hair like hers. My hair was very "Farrah"-like. The one thing I did do after seeing her was to make mine blonder. Farrah has great stories about it. We would be in her trailer, and when people would look at me they would say, "There's Farrah. There's Farrah." Obviously, they did not look at the face,

Q: *Why do gays love* Charlie's Angels?
A: Gay audiences have always have been seduced by glamour and sophistication. All the way back to the early black-and-white movies of Joan Crawford and

Mae West, a gay audience appreciates everything that goes into creating this kind of character, from the glamour, the makeup, to the hair. The way I see *Charlie's Angels* was an updated version of the good old black-and-white days because it was all about the hair, the clothes, and the makeup. It was not always about the storyline. It was more about what they looked like, what they were wearing and not wearing. Gays have a great eye for beauty and fashion, and they love all that.

The second season of *Charlie's Angels* included new angel Cheryl Ladd, Kate Jackson, and Jaclyn Smith.
(© Cynthia A. Lai)

CHAPTER FOUR

Why Do We Love *Charlie's Angels*?

1. The Hair

WHO DID not want Angel hair? Bigger was better, and it was really at its highest peak with Jill's full, fluffy, and feathered signature hairdo. Playing tennis or riding a skateboard, her hair was always ready for action.

Sabrina had a no-fuss overgrown pageboy that was just as practical as she was. Smart and sensible, this chic style always gave the criminals a run for their money.

Kelly possessed long, layered locks. When she wasn't running from a bomb, she was defusing one. And whether flipping her hair or the bad guy over her shoulder, this sharpshooter could bring anyone to his knees.

Kris won our hearts with her innocence and naiveté. Her hair was all one length, either pulled back or left down to frame her Angelic face. Even with knives being thrown at her, her style was still a cut above the rest.

Tiffany's side part gave an elegant charm to an educated Bostonian. No matter if she was stranded on a desert island or applying at a modeling agency, this Angel's look said it with class.

"I would finish a sixteen-something hour day, and then do wardrobe fittings on a script I hadn't even read, and then was picked up at 4:45 the next morning with my hair in rollers so it could be drying on the way to the set. They always think it's some big thrill to sit in the make-up chair for two hours to do hair and make-up. I would have had my hair in pigtails every show if I could."

—Farrah Fawcett

And whether wet or wild, Julie's kick-ass auburn hair was always ready for a bikini or an evening gown. In front of the camera or behind, this Angel's beauty was her most dangerous weapon.

---

2. The Cars

The Angels cars were so bitching! Jill's white Cobra with a blue stripe was just as sporty as she was. Kelly's tan mustang reflected her own classic style. And Sabrina's orange Pinto was as smart and dynamic as she was and flattered her turtlenecks so perfectly! Whether chasing after the bad guys or racing to have their hair done, these cars were as resilient as the characters.

---

3. The Chick Factor

The Angels were the cool friends we wanted to be around. They were well-coiffed and really knew how to take a bad boy down with a wink, a karate chop, or a flip of their hair. Regardless of which one was in jeopardy, they always had fun catching those bad guys. And shopping was always a must. Now we're talking heaven!

---

4. The Cases

The Angels found themselves working some of the most intriguing cases. From rescuing their kidnapped boss, whom they had never seen or met in person, in Hawaii, to stopping machine-gun-toting assassins from killing international political dignitaries, to tracking down rocket fuel hidden aboard an antique car, they were always ready to go to work when Charlie called.

Some of the covers they took were interesting, to say the least. Yet sometimes they had little or no covers at all. They were prostitutes, ladies of the night, hookers, call girls, escorts, masseuses (Oh, wait . . . those are all the same. Someone should have told the writers!). They were also racecar drivers, jewelry thieves, beauty contestants, cheerleaders, football players, clairvoyants, and even aliens from outer space. No matter what the cover, the Angels could do it.

Let's take the cult classic, "Angels in Chains." Who was in the pitch meeting for that one? The Angels get framed for drugs, are hauled off to prison, and are then made to strip down to their birthday suits and shower. After that, they are forced to dig potatoes during the day while turning tricks with the prison suppliers by night. And as an added touch, let's chain all three of them together. Now that's good TV. What a way to spend Wednesday nights!

---

5. The Teeny-Tiny Bikinis

From the moment Kelly emerged from a swimming pool in her infamous white bikini in the series pilot, the audience was craving more. To satisfy that hunger, Kelly, then Kris, and eventually Julie were put into predicaments that allowed them to show off their attractive assets. Whether going on a modeling shoot, vacationing at a mountain resort, training to be lifeguards, or shopping for groceries (I don't think that one happened!), this helped to raise the ratings. Whenever the ratings began to dip, the skin exposure went back up, among other things. Wow, puberty, what a time to remember!

Jill and Tiffany preferred the one-piece bathing suits that made us long for more. And sadly, Sabrina's sole bikini was burned in a cabin fire while cruising the high seas. That made for one *hot* bikini.

---

6. The Jiggle Effect

Stop, criminals, stop! Most of the time those darn criminals would just keep running. This meant that the Angels had to run after them, allowing their braless moneymakers to shake when they ran. Hence the term "Jiggle TV" was born. When working for Charles Townsend, bras were obviously optional. Those things just held the Angels back and were not flattering underneath their heavenly clothing! The show could have also been known as *Seven Boobs* (sorry, Bosley) *and a Squawk Box called Charlie*!

---

7. Locations

With offices in Los Angeles, Hawaii, and Paris, these Cherubs were flying all over the world and cruising into exotic locations to solve the latest case. There were kidnappings in Hawaii, stolen diamonds in the Caribbean, homicides in Las Vegas, drugs in Acapulco, death threats in Vail, frightened beauty contestants in Iowa, and disappearing inmates in Louisiana. However, these Angelic beauties always returned back to the City of Angels, which they called home.

"Aaron just loved my belly button. He liked me in crop tops and low-cut pants. Every time I showed my navel, he was happy. It was a compliment for a woman who had a two-year-old baby. I had whipped myself back into shape."

—Cheryl Ladd

"I remember Jaclyn and Cheryl saying, "Fantastic, Tanya, you can wear all the bathing suits. Throw them all on Tanya."

—Tanya Roberts

8. She-Devilish Villains

Our Angels were entangled with some very masculine-looking women. They were so mean, so matronly, and not very pretty. There was Bloody Mary the racecar driver ("Hellride," episode 1), Maxine the prison guard ("Angels in Chains," episode 4), Inga the masseuse ("The Killing Kind," episode 6), Bad Betty the roller derby skater ("Angels on Wheels," episode 12), Julia Smyth, owner of the Panthers football team ("Angels in the Backfield," episode 39), Dr. Slavin and Zora the masseuse ("Angels in Springtime," episode 50), and prison inmate Big Aggie ("Caged Angel," episode 74). No matter what the situation, the Angels always had each other to watch their backsides from any lesbian entanglements!

9. The Mysterious Charlie

Who wouldn't want to work for a millionaire boss whom you never have to see, but who communicates to you via speakerphone? That sounds like my kind of gig!

Charles Townsend had a deep, sincere voice you could trust. He was complimentary, generous, and compassionate. He also supplied the Angels with vehicles to drive and compensated them quite well. And no matter what, he was always a phone call away. With an employer like that, who wouldn't put her life in danger for him?

THE *REAL* TOWNSEND AGENCY

Ever wonder if the Charles Townsend Private Investigations really existed? Sorry, Charlie, it didn't. However, the building that they used for exterior shots does. It's located at 189 N. Robertson Boulevard, Beverly Hills, California. And it is presently the home of Miele, a high-end home appliance store.

The employees at Miele find it quite endearing when they see fans outside taking photos of the building. Most don't realize that they can also come inside. But don't expect the interior to resemble the studio set. If you're ever in the area, drop by and say that "Charlie" sent you!

And for you super-fans, did you realize that this is not Charlie's original office? The building exterior used in the pilot episode is located at 8619 Sunset Boulevard, West Hollywood, California. It has a white exterior with pillars. It looks virtually the same as it did back in 1976. And if you look closely, you might see Scott Woodville, the agency lawyer whose character was discontin-

Don't you think it's a bit odd that these super-smart detectives could never locate their millionaire boss? Every week they would work together to track down the bad guy, but never Charlie. Even more peculiar, a large percentage of the Angels' clients either knew

The Charles Townsend Private Investigations today. One can visit it on Robertson Boulevard in Beverly Hills, California. Say "Charlie" sent you! (© Mike Pingel)

ued, wandering around the building wondering where Bosley and the Angels disappeared to.

The agency building in the 2000 movie was made a bit larger than the original and built on the back lot of Universal Studios Hollywood. (They will show you where the building was during the "Hollywood Back Lot Tour")

Charlie or were friends with him. Yet no one was able to provide them with a recent picture of their mysterious boss.

Besides his professional side, Charlie also had a very private side. He enjoyed sipping cocktails while in the

HOLLYWOOD ANGELS

If you follow the path of stars on Hollywood Boulevard, you will be able to stumble across the Angels. No, not the actors from the show, but their sparkling stars on the Hollywood Walk of Fame. Farrah, Jaclyn, John, and producers Aaron and Leonard each have a star. In order to find them, you don't have to call Charlie. Instead, they are provided below:

Farrah Fawcett	7757 Hollywood Blvd, Hollywood, CA
Jaclyn Smith	7000 Hollywood Blvd, Hollywood, CA
Leonard Goldberg	6901 Hollywood Blvd, Hollywood, CA
Aaron Spelling	6667 Hollywood Blvd, Hollywood, CA
John Forsythe	6549 Hollywood Blvd, Hollywood, CA

company of scantily dressed women. Charlie took great pride in keeping all his girls happy and was always ready to rise to the occasion when needed. I'd like to tell you more, but sorry, Charlie, you've just been disconnected!

ANGELIC MUSEUM

South Dakota's own Cheryl Ladd is paid tribute via a display at the Dakotaland Museum, located at West 3rd Sreet on the State Fairgrounds, Huron, South Dakota. It features scrapbooks, posters, records, and many photos from her films. Previously, these items were on display at the Barn, a local restaurant where Cheryl worked as a carhop when she was a teenager. Unfortunately, due to progress, it no longer exists.

---

10. The Chase

After talking to Charlie, jetting off to exotic locales, prancing around in bikinis, jiggling and flipping their

HEAVENLY WEBSITES

Check out these official websites for Farrah Fawcett (www.farrahfawcett.us), Jaclyn Smith (www.jaclynsmith.com), and Cheryl Ladd (www.cherylladd.com).

If you would like to find out what projects the Angels are currently working on, go to www.charliesangels.com.

Angels' surfers should also check out these sites: www.chuckscherubs.com, www.myfarrah.com, www.kate-jackson.com, and www.angelwheels.net.

hair, one of the Angels always managed to get into jeopardy. Thank goodness the other two were there to track her down. It didn't matter if they had to steal a car, hijack a taxi, land an airplane, rummage through a car salvage yard, impersonate themselves, or help convicts escape from prison, they did whatever it took to get the criminal. And then the chase began, via automobile, horseback, bicycle, motorcycle, snowmobile, boat, skis, and even roller skates. Those poor lawbreakers just never stood a chance!

On Cloud Nine with Tanya Roberts

We were all together when that would happen. It was like we were on a conference call. We all would be laughing and talking, so it was really easy.—on acting to the speaker box

I had not been a fan of the show; I was not much of a television watcher. Barry and I had lived in New York; our interests were directed more toward live theater and foreign films. I knew about *Charlie's Angels* You would have to be dead or on another planet if you didn't.

I always saw the Angels as clean-cut, beautiful, model-type chicks. When I read the script, I saw they were going in a very different direction with the part. I came from a very cultured family, but I was a crazy rebel. I left home at sixteen and grew up by myself.

I thought, "Wow, this character is almost me, in a way." It was very different than the other Angels, she took care of herself and didn't put up with any bullshit. Julie was a very tough and in-your-face kind of girl.

I screen-tested twice for the show. When I first came in, my hair was very dark brown, including bangs, and I was wearing a high-collar blouse which didn't show much cleavage. Aaron didn't like it. He said, "We're going to change your hair and change your look." It was just the wrong outfit to wear for an Angels audition!

For the second screen test, they put me into some tight clothing with tons of cleavage and made my hair red. I loved the red, because I thought it brought my blue eyes out! Red was fine by me; I didn't mind it at all.

Aaron had told me there were three or four of us it came down to. He called me the night before and said, "Listen, we can't tell you if you got it now, but if you did, be sure you can be ready at 6 a.m., they will come and pick you up. Put you in full makeup and take pictures. So we'll call you at 6 a.m. if you got it." Of course I didn't sleep one wink.

Well, 6 a.m. rolled around and the phone rang, and a limo was outside my door at 7 a.m. That was the beginning of when the whole insanity started. I was news! I was introduced to the press that morning as the new Angel and Bam! doing my first photo shoot. My very first one-on-one interview was with Rona Barrett, who was huge at that time.

The hardest thing was the immediate fame, which I sincerely felt at the time that I didn't deserve. To get famous for doing nothing was unexpected. You expect to earn fame, work hard and eventually do some movies and then have a hit. But you don't expect overnight the whole world to be taking pictures everywhere you go. I was not very comfortable about it for a lot of years. You're raised to believe you need to pay your dues and that just doesn't happen in Hollywood. At first I was very freaked by it.

When I got the part, we immediately flew to Hawaii, and then the actors strike happened. The strike took three months. Even though our show had OK ratings, the strike brought the end of the show sooner. Back then shows fulfilled their five-year contract and moved on, not like today when a show can go on forever. I knew coming into it, that it wasn't going any further than the year.

The day the show was cancelled, we were all on set, and the head executives came down. Aaron announced this was it and we were not going on for another season. I was crushed, but Cheryl and Jaclyn were jumping up and down with joy! I said, "Come on, guys, lets do another season," and they both said, "NO WAY."

The show gave me a lot of visibility and opened doors for more work. *Angels* was a first-class production, and those were some fun days.

Season four cast with Jaclyn Smith, Cheryl Ladd, and new Angel Shelley Hack. (© American Broadcasting Companies, Inc.)

CHAPTER FIVE

The Angels' Backgrounds

THE BACKGROUNDS are compiled from the episodes. However, not all the information correlates due to facts being changed to fit the storylines.

Sabrina Duncan, the "Smart Angel"

Background

Sabrina was born in Philadelphia, Pennsylvania. She grew up the daughter of a general in the Army. In high school she was a cheerleader. While in college, she majored in political science. After college she decided to enroll in the Los Angeles Police Academy. During that time, she met, married, and divorced fellow police officer Bill Duncan. She also became best friends with fellow rookies Jill Munroe and Kelly Garrett. All three were offered jobs as private detectives for Charles Townsend Private Investigations. After three years of working for Charlie, she left to get married and was expecting a baby.

Detective Style

As a detective, Sabrina was known for her undercover character work as a racecar driver, clairvoyant, wanted criminal, bag lady, horse jockey, French clothing designer, football player, prostitute, Keystone Cop, mime, and maid. She even had to pose as an imposter of herself! And at times she would come up with better ideas than Charlie on how to crack the case.

Personal Style

Sabrina preferred a low-maintenance style from her short, straight hair all the way down to her turtlenecks and blue jeans. However, being the consummate professional, this Angel would wear suits or evening gowns when needed. And she really knew how to make an explosive entrance when she wore her "boom-boom" belt.

Residence

Sabrina resides in a spacious condo in Century City, California.

Jill Munroe, the "Athletic Angel"

Background

Jill was born and raised in Los Angeles, California, along with her kid sister Kris, by their alcoholic father. Growing up, she was very athletic and into sports. In college, she was a champion swimmer with a very strong final kick. After college she enrolled in the Los Angeles

Police Academy. During that time, she became best friends with fellow rookies Kelly Garrett and Sabrina Duncan. All three were offered jobs as private detectives for Charles Townsend Private Investigations. A year later, she left the Townsend agency to pursue her dream of becoming a racecar driver. She went on to become the first woman to win Le Mans and later the Grand Prix. While competing, she met and became engaged to fellow racecar driver Steve Carmody. However, the engagement was short-lived when Steve was killed in an explosion when he was test-driving a racecar for Jill. Eventually, she returned to racecar driving. And whenever she is in town, she lends the Angels a helping hand in solving their latest case.

Detective Style

As a detective, Jill incorporated her love of sports into her work. These athletic attributes assisted her with covers as a tennis pro, swimmer, dance instructor, masseuse, roller derby skater, jewel thief, prostitute, nurse, gambler, model, and centerfold. And no matter what, this Angel knew how to skateboard her way out of any difficult situation.

Personal Style

Jill was blessed with California good looks and a mane of golden, cascading hair. Whether she was all dressed up, in a pair of jeans, or just wearing a towel, Jill always looked fantastic. And she could make even the hardest criminal purr whenever she would prance around as a "feline." Meow!

Residence

Jill resides in a waterfront home in Malibu, California.

Kelly Garrett, the "Streetwise Angel"

Background

As an infant, Kelly was an orphan and spent her early childhood at the St. Agnes Orphanage in Houston, Texas. There she was abused by a matron named Beamish, and her sole friend at the time was her doll Lillibet. Eventually, she moved in with a foster family, who brought her out to Los Angeles. However, things didn't work out, and she was forced to live in an orphanage when she wasn't being passed around from one foster family to another. Growing up on the streets of Los Angeles, Kelly turned into a rebel and was always getting in trouble. Not liking the direction her life was heading, she straightened herself out and enrolled in the Los Angeles Police Academy. While there, she became best friends with fellow rookies Sabrina Duncan and Jill Munroe. All three were offered jobs as private detectives for Charles Townsend Private Investigations. Kelly still works for the agency.

Detective Style

As a detective, Kelly's checkered past gave her an edge but also made her very sensitive. She would go out of her way to aid any child in danger. Regardless of her undercover work as a beauty contestant, nun, cheerleader, horticulturalist, model, cruise director, singer, jewel thief, belly dancer, alien from outer space, Vegas showgirl, or stuntwoman, this Angel could make any criminal stop in his tracks.

Personal Style

As a classic beauty with long, layered hair, Kelly's style matched her persona. She could wear a jumpsuit, bikini, evening gown or even a towel, and still exude class. And this Angel could give any man a run for his money whether she was picking a lock, giving a karate chop, or shooting a machine gun.

Residence

Kelly resides in a home in Century City, California.

Kris Munroe, the "Rookie Angel"

Background

Kris was born and raised in Los Angeles, California, along with her older sister Jill, by their alcoholic father. Growing up, she spent her summers in Arizona with her Aunt Lydia and Uncle Paul and went by the nickname of "Sweet Kristmas." After she finished high school, Jill decided to send Kris through college. There she had aspirations of becoming an actress. Her first professional acting job was in summer stock theater as "Jenny" in the musical *Sweet Misery.* After a short period in college, Kris decided to follow in her sister's footsteps by secretly enrolling herself in the San Francisco Police Academy. After graduating, Kris was asked to join

Charles Townsend Private Investigations after her sister Jill had recently left to fulfill her dream of becoming a racecar driver. Kris accepted the position and still continues to work for the agency.

Detective Style

As a detective, Kris started out a little green, making many mistakes. As her confidence increased, so did her professionalism. With skillful determination, she was able to handle covers as a showgirl, disco dancer, beauty contestant, truck driver, singer, biker chick, jewel thief, porn star, real estate agent, exercise instructor, prostitute, ice-skating clown, model, and cheerleader. And at a drop of a hat, she was willing to jump into a swamp and wrestle with alligators.

Personal Style

With long, blonde hair, Kris was as fun and carefree as her sister Jill, and had the taste in clothing to match. From an evening gown, jeans, or a bikini, to a palm leaf or absolutely nothing at all, she could accentuate her attributes and really make them shine. And she could make a rabbit stew to curl your toes!

Residence

Kris resides in a waterfront home in Pacific Cove, California.

Tiffany Welles, the "Sophisticated Angel"

Background

Tiffany was born in Boston, Massachusetts, and was raised by her police officer father and Latin teacher mother. After high school, she attended Whitley College and was president of her sorority, Kappa Omega Psi. During one of her summer breaks, she tapped into her psychic abilities while working for a famous ghost hunter. Upon finishing college, she decided to follow in her father's footsteps. She attended and graduated from the Boston Police Academy at the top of her class. Afterwards, Tiffany was offered a position working for her father's childhood friend, Charlie Townsend. After only one year at the Charles Townsend Private Investigations, Tiffany left the agency and decided to stay back East for a while.

Detective Style

As a detective, Tiffany was very well educated. No matter what role she took on, whether posing as a truck driver, pest exterminator, nun, prostitute, psychic, model, nurse, or violinist, this Angel could blend in convincingly. And she makes the most delectable chocolate chip cookies.

Personal Style

With her asymmetrical hairstyle, straight or curly, Tiffany was on the cutting edge. She had a high fashion sense that brought new sophistication to Charlie's trio. Goodbye bell-bottoms, hello glamour!

Residence

Tiffany resided in a lovely two-story home in Studio City, California, before going back East. The former owners of this house were Darrin and Samantha Stephens, who were known to be a very bewitching couple.

Julie Rogers, the "Model Angel"

Background

Julie was born in New York City and was raised by her alcoholic mother. Growing up on the streets, she had a very troubled life. As a teenager she was involved in street scuffles and disturbing the peace. At twenty-four, she was caught shoplifting and was sentenced to six months in a correctional facility. After her release, she turned her life around and became a model at the Woodman Modeling Agency. While there, she noticed the drug scene and reported this information back to her parole officer and best friend, Harry Stearns.

When her roommate is murdered, she crosses paths with Kelly Garrett and Kris Munroe, who are investigating her roommate's death. After Harry is shot and killed, Julie joins forces with the Angels to find out who is behind the murders. As the case concludes, Julie joins the Charles Townsend Private Investigations team and is given a temporary detective license.

Detective Style

As a detective, Julie's rough upbringing gave her a helping hand in reading people. No matter if she was a photographer, lifeguard, go-go dancer, waitress, or stuntwoman, this Angel knew how to take control of the situation.

Personal Style

As a former model with shoulder length layered hair, Julie looked good in everything and was most confident in a bikini. I bet this Angel could balance a book on her head while running in heels!

Residence

Julie resides in an apartment in Marina Del Ray, California.

John Bosley "The Teddy Bear"

Background

While attending college, Bosley showed his youthful exuberance by skinny-dipping. He was eventually hired to work for Charles Townsend Private Investigations and assisted in recruiting the Angels. He was married briefly and occasionally dates but confesses that he is married to his work. He considers his family to be Charlie, the Angels, and his pet cocker spaniel. And once a week he makes time to play bridge with his good friend Claire.

David Doyle with his wife and a fan in Hawaii during filming of "Angels in Paradise." Check out the fan's T-shirt! So heavenly! (© Cynthia A. Lai)

Detective Style

As Charlie's facilitator, Bosley watches over the Angels and is the all-around comic relief. He always hopes to get out of the office and accompany the girls out in the field, but paperwork generally keeps him behind. However, he has had the opportunity to assist the Angels with a variety of covers, including a preacher, birdwatcher, mobster, magician/mind reader, diamond thief, model, bartender, chauffeur, and keystone cop. And in one memorable moment, he was even knocked out and stripped naked—talk about having no cover at all!

Personal Style

With his slicked-back hair, Bosley was known for his professional attire, which generally consisted of slacks, sports jacket, and tie. On occasion, or when working out of the office in Hawaii, Bosley could be spotted wearing casual clothes. But he had to be extra-careful while undercover, because his wife has been known to pack brown shoes with a black tuxedo.

Residence

Bosley resides in Los Angeles, California.

The Artist and Muse

Farrah Fawcett is more than a gorgeous woman whose infamous swimsuit poster hung on millions of walls; she is also an artist with a great talent for painting, drawing, and sculpting. She has been creating art since her days at the University of Texas. In 1998, Fawcett showcased her artistic talents in her DVD (also on pay-per-view), *All of Me.*

In 2002, she began sculpting with Keith Edmier. Every step of their artistic endeavor was photographed for their book, *Keith Edmier and Farrah Fawcett: Recasting Pygmalion,* by author Lynn Zelevansky. Their final sculptures were displayed at the Los Angeles County Museum of Art. The exhibition was titled Contemporary Projects 7: Keith Edmier and Farrah Fawcett 2000.

Fawcett also inspired many artists as well. Andy Warhol painted her. The country band Alabama wrote a song about her, "She's Got That Look in Her Eyes." Super Deluxe released a song named after her, "Farrah Fawcett." Lee Majors sang about her in the opening credits of *The Fall Guy.* And Carlos Franzetti featured her on the cover of his record, *Graffiti.*

HEAVENLY TIDBITS

Air, the popular French band, wrote "Kelly Watch the Stars" in 1998 as a tribute to their favorite Angel, Kelly Garrett (Jaclyn Smith).

Angel Love

In 1982, Kate Jackson, Michael Ontkean, and Harry Hamlin starred in *Making Love,* a gay coming-out love story that centers around a married man who realizes after eight years of marriage that he has desires to be with a man. This was first time a mainstream film showcased a gay man coming to terms with his homosexuality.

An Angel's Empire

After endorsing many well-known products, such as Breck, Wella Balsam, and Max Factor, Jaclyn Smith joined forces with Kmart in 1985 to create fashionable clothing at affordable prices. Her signature line has blossomed into accessories, including shoes, purses, and jewelry.

In 1989, she and Max Factor created her signature fragrance, Jaclyn Smith's California, the fragrance that captures the dream.

And in 2002, she took her love of designs even further, creating her own furniture line, Jaclyn Smith's Home. The line includes furnishings for the living room, dining room, and bedroom.

"I feel really great about it. It's been over twenty years now and it has made over $11 billion. I did what I set out to do, which was to give quality, stylish clothes at good, affordable prices. I was first at branding. Now it's more than just a celebrity brand; it's a true brand. It's held its own through the ups and downs of Kmart. It's one of my accomplishments that I'm really proud of. The clothes have loyal customers that come back because they know what the line represents. I'm grateful for it and their extreme loyalty to my line."

—Jaclyn Smith

CELEBRITY SURVEY #3: WHO IS YOUR FAVORITE ANGEL?

"Kelly is probably my favorite Angel. She was always there, and always calm."

—John August, screenwriter, *Charlie's Angels, Charlie's Angels: Full Throttle, Go*

"That's like Sophie's Choice—I could never decide."

—Peter Paige, actor, *Queer as Folk*

"Farrah Fawcett—just because of the poster. That was the first time I ever saw a woman with hard nipples."

—ANT, comedian, actor, *Last Comic Standing*

"I was already a big fan of Kate from *The Rookies* and found her face extremely appealing. I like the idea of casting her as a brainy, bespectacled Angel with short hair to offset the two bombshells. But I'd have to say that looks-wise, Jaclyn is my favorite. Her face is so perfect that she'd be considered a great beauty in any time period, and she really required very little makeup. She's like a sexy doll or Valerie Bertinelli's hot aunt. And Jaclyn still looks sensational today."

—Lady Bunny, ladybunny.net

"I had crushes on Jill, Kelly, and Kris. After that there were no more "real" Angels, only fillers. I could go there with Kris because she was Jill's little sister, but after that, all the wanna-be Angels just got ridiculous. Shelley Hack? Seriously? Give me a break. Tanya Roberts??? No way. My favorite of those three? Hmmm. Rough. Kris and Kelly. Can I have two? Please?"

—Michelle Wolff, actress, *Dante's Cove*

"I simply adore Jaclyn "Kelly Garrett" Smith. She is, was, and will always be stunning and she seems so sweet. I would be just crushed to learn that she's a total bitch. Also, she's got her own line of fashionable, yet affordable, clothing at K-Mart!"

—Jackie Beat, jackiebeatreal.com

"I did and I do. It happens to be Jaclyn Smith, Kelly Garrett. I'm sure she is the favorite of many. There was something always about her that I found graceful. She seemed too pretty for the job, which is what I loved about the show to begin with. It had so many wrongs which made it right. That is why she was my favorite. She was just fabulous! She was a runway model detective."

—Oscar Quintero, creator of *Chico's Angels*

"Farrah. She went off the show so fast and had so much scandal that followed her. I wanted all the scandal to disappear and really wanted her to come back.

She had great hair. People made fun of her acting. Then she did *The Burning Bed*. She was so frickin' fabulous in it and got nominated for an Emmy. She was so successful after leaving *Charlie's Angels* and was so dogged in the press. That is why I love her so much."

—Chi Chi LaRue, director, Channel 1 Releasing

"I know it's typical, but Jill, hands down. Farrah Fawcett-Majors was a living special effect!"

—Glen Hanson, artist, www.glenhanson.com

"I liked Jill's jiggly sex appeal and Kelly's drop-dead gorgeousness, but my favorite Angel was Sabrina. She was a little plainer, a little smarter, a bit more lesbian, really. And, to think, with all that going for her, she still ended up married to a gay guy in *Making Love*."

—Frank DeCaro, host, *The Frank DeCaro Show* on Sirius

"My favorite is Jill. Farrah Fawcett was just sex on a stick at that time. And you watched her, just trying to figure out her secrets. She had plenty. The big fluffy hair. The poster of her nipples—not that you saw them on the show, but you watched the show knowing she'd let the world get a little glimpse of them. Her constant big smile (something Julia Roberts has obviously copied and I'm really sick of it now) and her cute Texas accent. She was one kick-ass woman."

—Julie Brown, comedian, actress, singer, www.juliebrown.com

"Tiffany Welles is my favorite. I dig Tiffany. She was tall, wore spandex, and she never left Bosley's side. She really didn't do very much. I kind of felt sorry for her."

—Dylan Vox, actor, *The Lair*

The Singing Angel

Singing is what brought Cheryl Ladd to Los Angeles as she toured with the band the Music Shop. After they arrived the band dissolved, and she moved forward with her singing career. She was cast as the singing voice of Melody in the Saturday morning TV cartoon *Josie and the Pussycats.* The stars of that show recorded one album and planned to go out on tour, which never happened.

When she joined the cast of *Charlie's Angels,* she was able to showcase her singing talent in the episode "Angels in the Wings" and then in "Angels in Vegas."

After she became an international star on the series, she signed and recorded four albums under Capital Records. Her song "Think It Over" went on to become a pop hit, breaking into the top 40 in the United States. It was in Japan where Ladd was most successful: each of her four albums went gold there.

In 2000, Cheryl Ladd hit the Broadway stage, replacing Reba McEntire in the musical revival of *Annie Get Your Gun.*

The Three Gay Angels

Tab Hunter, Robert Reed, and Dick Sargent all played against type when they guest-starred on *Charlie's Angels.*

Little did these leading men know at that time just how much of an impact they would eventually have on gay culture.

Tab Hunter, "Nips and Tucks" (episode #89)

Hunter portrays on-the-run mobster Bill Maddox, who is in dire need of plastic surgery in order to escape the United States without being recognized.

Tab Hunter began his career as a teen idol and singer. His first acting role was in *The Lawless*. He went on to work in the film version of *Damn Yankees* and was nominated for an Oscar. He has appeared in over fifty films, including *Polyester* and *Grease 2*. His number 1 hit song, "Young Love," topped the Billboard charts for six weeks in 1957.

In 2005 Hunter wrote his autobiography, *Tab Hunter Confidential: The Making of a Movie Star*. In the pages of the book he acknowledged his homosexuality, which confirmed all those rumors that had been circulating since his teenage years. Hunter has been with his partner Allan Glaser for over twenty-five years.

Robert Reed, "One Love . . . Two Angels" (episodes #92 and #93)

Reed plays Glenn Staley, the scheming nephew of multimillionaire Oliver Barrows. Staley plots an elaborate plan to kill his uncle and his newfound daughter Kelly Garrett in order to get control of Barrows's estate.

Robert Reed is best known for giving groovy advice as Mike Brady on *The Brady Bunch*. He went on to reprise his fatherly role in *The Brady Bunch Hour, The Brady Brides* and *The Bradys*. Reed was once married briefly to Marilyn Rosenberg and has a daughter, Caroline Reed.

Reed never officially came out of the closet and struggled with his homosexuality throughout his life. He contracted HIV and died of colorectal cancer with complications related to AIDS. Days before his passing, he contacted his TV wife, Florence Henderson, to have her inform the "Brady kids" of his condition. He passed away in 1992.

Dick Sargent

Sargent was an Angel casting favorite, showing up on the series three times.

"Angels on Wheels" (episode #12)
Sargent plays Hugh Morris, owner of an insurance company that heavily insured his own female roller derby team, the Tornadoes.

"Angels in Vegas" (episode #47)
Sargent portrays Marty Cole, a lounge singer who gaslights his boss, Frank Howell, in retaliation, after Cole's wife's death.

"Love Boat Angels" (Episode #69)
Sargent plays insurance broker James Avery, who hires the Angels to find $5 million in stolen antiques.

Wiggle your nose and see who pops up! Dick Sargent, who was known by millions of devoted *Bewitched*

"I think back in the day, when the show came out, there were not really any gay people on television. But the coolness of the chicks—they're pretty much gay guys. They were like bad asses but they had that cool air of sophistication. They drove really cool-ass cars like Cobras, Mustangs, and Pintos."

—Dylan Fox, *The Lair*

fans as Darrin Stevens, the husband of Samantha, the witch with a funny twitch! He went on to do numerous guest appearances on TV shows in the 1970s and 1980s, and costarred in the sitcom *Down to Earth* in 1984.

In 1991, he came out publicly about being gay after a tabloid story claimed he had AIDS. From then on, he became a role model for the gay community and was vocal about gay rights. He and his former *Bewitched* costar Elizabeth Montgomery were co-Grand Marshals of the Los Angeles Gay Pride Parade in 1992. Sadly, Sargent passed away in 1994, after his long battle with prostate cancer. He is survived by his life partner Albert Williams.

Jaclyn Smith, Farrah Fawcett, and Kate Jackson all chained up and nowhere to run in the cult classic episode "Angels in Chains." (© American Broadcasting Companies, Inc.)

CHAPTER SIX

Q Case Files

BOZ HAS gone through the Townsend files to share some of the most exciting cases!

Season One

The Pilot (90-minute movie)

Airdate: March 21, 1976
Writers: Ivan Goff and Ben Roberts
Directed by: John Llewellyn Moxey

Case Plot

Vincent LeMaire, a wealthy vineyard owner, has been missing for seven years and is about to be pronounced legally dead. His estate is supposed to go to his only daughter, Janet, whose whereabouts are unknown. If

The Case File Breakdowns: Season One, 1976–1977

Angels	*Airtime*	*Final Rating*	*Cost per Episode*
Sabrina Duncan Jill Munroe Kelly Garrett John Bosley	Wednesday 10 p.m.–11 p.m. EST/PST	5	$310,000

she does not show up to claim her inheritance, the estate will go to Vincent's second wife, Rachel. The Angels are hired to find out what really happened to Vincent LeMaire.

Kelly shows up at the winery posing as Janet. Feeling threatened by the potential loss of the estate, Rachel, with the assistance of Bo Creel, serves Kelly milk laced with poison.

After hearing a knock on the door, Rachel finds outs from attorney Scott Woodville that the woman posing as Janet LeMaire is an imposter and that the real Janet is on her way. Kelly does not drink the poison milk and shows up alive and explains she helped to kidnap the real Janet. She proceeds to blackmail Bo and Rachel into helping her claim $20 million worth of the estate.

Sabrina appears as the real Janet and sets up the bait by pretending to want worthless swampland for a bird sanctuary. Having previously sold the swampland, Rachel and Bo have to buy the land back. The Angels are then captured as they watch Bo retrieve the dead body of Vincent LeMaire from his watery grave. Thanks to Charlie tipping off Aram Kolegian, the police arrive, and the Angels escape to safety. It is safe for Janet LeMaire to return home and claim her inheritance.

Tidbits

The ninety-minute film was the basis for the TV show. In this pilot, the Angels were written as detectives, but that confused the preview audience. The writers came up with the concept that they were former police officers to help explain their backgrounds. This was the only case during which the Angels did not use their guns. And two men were not needed as liaisons for Charlie, so the character of Scott Woodville was eliminated.

Musical Moment

Whenever the Angels appeared, music played. It was integrated into the series for first few years but then tapered off.

Celestial Hunk Alert

Tommy Lee Jones guest-starred as Aram Kolegian, a childhood friend of Janet LeMaire. Jones went on to a very successful film career in such mega-hits as *Men in Black* and *Double Jeopardy* and won the 1993 Oscar for Best Actor in a Supporting Role for his work in *The Fugitive.*

Bo Hopkins played bad guy Bo Creel. Hopkins later guest-starred in a second *Charlie's Angels* episode, "Love Boat Angels" (episode #69). Eventually he would go on to play Mathew Blaisdel in the miniseries *Oil* for Aaron Spelling, which turned into the TV series *Dynasty.*

Comments

Aaron Spelling's home was used for exterior shots of Kelly coming out of the swimming pool, Jill playing tennis, and Charlie being served a drink while soaking in a Jacuzzi.

Angel Memory: Farrah Fawcett

"I remember vividly filming the swamp scene. They said, 'Just get in the swamp, Farrah, and go under the water.'

Farrah Fawcett with a police escort to the set of *Charlie's Angels* in 1977 due to threats from stalkers. (©catrescue@monmouth.com/Nancy Barr-Brandon)

It was freezing cold. I remember the water was dirty and they kept saying, 'Go under. Go all the way under; we can see the little top of your cap.' When I came out of the water, they went, 'Well, can you take that cap off so your hair looks good?' 'Oh, sure, no problem! So I did what they wanted and they said, 'Put the knit cap back on.' That water was freezing!"

Celestial Memories of Bo Hopkins

"When we threw the 'body' into the water, we couldn't pick it up, so everyone started laughing because it was heavier than we thought. We almost turned over (in the boat) three times and then finally they had to take some of the stuffing out of the 'body.'

"In the mornings I would come in and laugh with Diana Muldaur: we would listen to the wardrobe people, and they [Angels] would say, 'I want to wear that' and 'But I had this on somewhere the other day.' I laughed and said, 'This will never go'—they will never get the clothes right!"

Episode #2: "Hellride"

Written by: Edward J. Lakso
Director: Richard Lang
Airdate: September 22, 1976

Case Plot

The Angels go undercover to find out who has killed a female racecar driver. Sabrina takes to the track as one of the drivers, Jill and Bosley ride into town as Brother John and his lovely daughter, and Kelly becomes a track groupie. They uncover plans for a diamond heist that lead them into a high-speed race across the Mexican border.

Tidbit

Kate Jackson performed all her own stunt driving in this episode.

Gayest Moment

When Jill is collecting donations for the Lord, one of the suspects asks her what denomination she is. She responds with "35-24-35." Brother! Oh, we see the light!

Villain

Bloody Mary, played by Jenny O'Hara, set the standard of the "bad girl" role on *Charlie's Angels.* She is ruthless and does not take any crap from anyone. She is the Angels' first introduction to mean masculine women who will be pitted against them for the next five years.

Angel Memory: Farrah Fawcett

"I must have done that 'Angel praying hands' pose in every show. People have showed me so many photos of myself doing that."

Episode #3: "Night of the Strangler"

Written by: Pat Fielder
Story by: Pat Fielder, Glen Olson, and Rod Baker
Director: Richard Lang
Airdate: October 13, 1976

Case Plot

After a world-famous model has been strangled, the Angels are sent into the world of high-fashion modeling to find out who is behind the attack. At St. Clair, Inc., Jill and Kelly pose as models, leaving Sabrina to con her way in by pretending to be a photo stylist.

When a second model is strangled and an attempt is made on a third one, the Angels become totally puzzled.

I'M IN THE SHOWER, CHARLIE

"Magic Fire": Talk about *hot*! After performing feats of magic at the Magic Castle, Kris decides to take a shower. But instead of water, only hot, fiery flames come out. Which is hotter . . . Kris wrapped in a towel or the flames?

- "The Mexican Connection": Is that Jill being bad with someone in the shower? Oh, yes! But it's no gentleman caller; it's Kelly. She's helping Jill fight off the advances of a suspect. Jill really knows how to make her towel sizzle!
- "Angels in Chains": Who knew a scene with three girls showering would make such a stir in the world of TV . . . but with Sabrina, Jill and Kelly soaping up, it made this episode of the series a cult classic. How long has it been since you've been sprayed?
- "Angel in Love": While reviewing the case, the Angels are stripped down and rub elbows in a Jacuzzi. Is it me, or is it getting hot in here? And which one of you is making all those bubbles?
- "Angels on Campus": Tiffany is prancing around in a towel after taking a refreshing shower. However, danger lurks around the corner when she is locked in the locker room. Is that a tranquilizing dart in your pocket, or are you happy to see me?

The main suspect for each assault has an alibi for the other two attacks.

Eventually they discover that the three main suspects were working together in order to collect on an insurance policy on one their victims.

Gayest Moment

One of the best scenes in this episode is watching Sabrina throw sexual advances at Alec Witt. Just as things begin to get rough, Kelly arrives unexpectedly. Seeing Alec in the arms of another woman, she slaps him across the face. After an exchange of words among the three, Sabrina and Kelly storm out, but not before Kelly smacks Alec across the face one last time.

Mega-famous Star Alert

Richard Mulligan played lead character Kevin St. Clair. He went on to star in the comedy series *Soap* and *Empty Nest,* which was a spin-off from *The Golden Girls.* He won two Emmys for his work on both series and received a star on the Hollywood Walk of Fame in 1994.

Alley Cat Alert

The highlight of this episode is the catfight between Michelle St. Clair (Rosemary Forsyth) and Kelly. After seeing Kelly in the white bikini that she was supposed to wear, Michelle's teeth and claws come out as she pounces on Kelly. Chairs go flying. Hair is whipping around in every direction. The scuffle continues until Kelly finally pushes Michelle into the swimming pool to cool her off.

Episode #4: "Angels in Chains"

Written by: Robert Earll
Director: Phil Bondelli
Airdate: October 20, 1976

Case Plot

The Angels head off to prison to investigate the disappearance of a female inmate. After arriving in Pine Parish, Louisiana, they get arrested for possession of drugs. As they are hauled off to prison, they are forced to work in the potato fields by day and entertain prison suppliers at night. But after their cover is busted, they are chained together and taken to a nearby swamp to be killed. While fleeing via a truck loaded with potatoes, the trio escape harm by throwing potatoes at the pursuing police vehicle. Mashed potatoes, anyone?

Tidbit

"Angels in Chains" is a cult classic. Besides being the number 1 favorite episode among fans, it's also the one everybody remembers. And it's even Farrah Fawcett's favorite due to the fact that they did not have to have their hair and makeup done for a week; they just had to wet their hair!

Gayest Moment

The Angels are forced to strip down, take a shower, and then get sprayed for lice by a very masculine female prison guard.

Cherub Guest Star Alert

Actress Kim Basinger guest-starred as female inmate Linda Oliver. After being released from prison, Bosley hires her as the agency's new secretary. Unfortunately, the part was never written into subsequent episodes. The following year, Basinger was rumored to be the front-runner to replace Farrah Fawcett. She went on to win the 1997 Oscar for her role in *L.A. Confidential.*

Actress Lauren Tewes guest-starred as Christine Hunter, the woman who hired the Angels to find her missing sister. In 1977, Tewes went on to play cruise director Julie McCoy on the Aaron Spelling TV series *The Love Boat.* She sailed with the show until her dismissal over her public battle with cocaine in 1984. She eventually returned to the series in 1986. And in 1998, she reprised her character of Julie McCoy for *Love Boat: The Next Wave.*

Angel Memory: Farrah Fawcett

"My favorite outfit was the prison Levi's jeans and a denim shirt in 'Angels in Chains.' First of all, it was easy and required no long fittings, and it was my idea to keep our hair wet most of the time because it was so easy and we could use our energy to establish our growing camaraderie on the show. The worst outfit, which was also in the same episode, was that blue strapless prostitute dress.

"One thing I liked about filming 'Angels in Chains' is we got to focus on the camaraderie between the girls. That's when I suggested that we do more of that, and they went, 'No, no, no, no, no, no. no. We have a formula that works.' To save time I finally got the producers to let us play most of the time with wet hair. I loved that!"

Angel Memory: Jaclyn Smith

"The prison show was one of the high points for me. At that point we knew the show was a hit, and it was fun. I so clearly remember it, maybe because we were chained together."

Angel Memory: Leonard Goldberg

"'Angels in Chains' is my favorite episode for several reasons. First of all, after showing the pilot to ABC, the management asked a typical question, 'What would future episodes be like?' I gave them a rough outline of 'Angels in Chains,' and they interrupted me to say "We're buying the series." Second, it was the highest-rated episode of *Charlie's Angels* (I believe). And third, when the episode was going to air the *New York Times* ran a huge picture of the three girls chained together emerging from a swamp in their Sunday Arts and Leisure section."

Celestial Hunk Alert—Episode #5: Tom Selleck in "Target: Angels"

Airdate: October 27, 1976

Tom Selleck plays Kelly Garrett's boyfriend, Dr. Alan Samuelson. After Kelly becomes a target for a professional hit man, she pushes him away. One push is all it took. What a wimp! Selleck went on to play Thomas Sullivan Magnum IV, Hawaii's number 1 private eye on *Magnum, P.I.* Later he played Dr. Richard Burke, the boyfriend of Monica on the mega-hit *Friends.* In 2007, he took over the Montecito on NBC's *Las Vegas,* which also stars Cheryl Ladd.

Tidbits

It is a little known fact that both Fawcett and Selleck appeared in the 1970 movie *Myra Breckinridge* and in a commercial for Dubonnet liquor.

Angel Memory: Jaclyn Smith

"Tom Selleck was a very good kisser. What you would expect?"

Episode #8: "Lady Killer"

Written by: Sue Milburn
Directed: George McCowan
Airdate: November 24, 1976

Case Plot

Centerfolds from *Feline* magazine are being trimmed by murder. In each case, after they were killed, they also had all their hair cut off. Jill goes undercover as an up-and-coming centerfold, while Kelly sings to her heart's content as a lounge singer, leaving Sabrina to play "house" with the client, Tony Mann.

After the suspect list dwindles, Sabrina realizes the killer could be Tony's assistant Paula. Jill is unknowingly drugged by Paula and is set to become the next victim. Sabrina and Kelly race against time to save Jill from getting a deadly haircut.

Tidbits

The story line became reality in 1995, when Farrah Fawcett posed nude for *Playboy.* It was the best-selling issue of the magazine in the 1990s. In 1997, Fawcett posed once again, in the first issue to have two different covers released at the same time. Footage from both photo shoots, combined with some of Fawcett's creative ideas, were released to pay-per-view and on DVD as *All of Me*.

And Kate Jackson's future *Scarecrow and Mrs. King* costar, Martha Smith, guest-starred as the first feline to be murdered.

Gayest Moment

As she's entering Tony Mann's bedroom, Sabrina looks down and spots a microscopic wire attached to Tony's bed frame. As she follows the wire, she discovers that it connects to an electrical outlet. Sabrina throws an item at the frame, and the bed catches on fire. That's one quick way to get to heaven!

Cherub Guest Star Alert—Episode #10: Laurette Spang in "Consenting Adults"

Airdate: December 8, 1976

Laurette Spang played Dolores Martin, a.k.a. Tracy Martel, a college student by day, a professional hooker by night, and a part-time thief when time allowed! Spang is best known as Cassiopeia in the 1970s sci-fi TV series *Battlestar Galactica*.

Episode #11: "The Séance"

Written by: Roberts C Dennis

Director: George Brooke

Airdate: December 15, 1976

S&M ANGELS

No matter what case they were working on, it was a rule of thumb that generally one Angel always found herself in some form of peril. Eventually she'll get kidnapped. And if she's really lucky, she'll find herself bound and gagged.

If you like being tied up, check out these episodes.

- "Consenting Adults": After being bound and blindfolded, bullets fly by Sabrina's head, killing two other people in a warehouse. Lesson learned . . . if you see no evil, then no harm can come to you.
- "Pretty Angels in a Row": After getting nabbed in the trunk of car (Where else would an Angel hide inconspicuously?), Sabrina is captured and held for a heavenly ransom. So, is that an Angel in your trunk, or is the devil hiding out in your engine?
- "Magic Fire": Sabrina manages to get tied to a chair as a pyromaniac rigs a phone to start a fire. Thank goodness the Great Zolton (Bosley) uses his power of awareness to save Sabrina from a fiery death. There may not always be a side of beef lying around, but at least he knows which barnyard to pluck from.
- "Angels on the Air": Sabrina's cover is exposed as she is caught in a lie. After

being strapped down to a table, she is threatened with injection of a truth serum. Wouldn't washing her mouth out with soap be easier?

- "Angels Ahoy": Kelly is given a swimming lesson with hands tied behind her back while wearing a tutu. After being doused with alcohol, she is pushed into the pool. After she floats to the top, she politely asks her captors to use nets to push her back down. When that didn't work, she had her coworkers kick her captors' asses.
- "An Angel's Trail": What rotten luck Jill has when she finds herself tied up, forced to ride around in a beat-up van on her way to the Canadian border, and having to sit next to characters right out of Steinbeck's *Of Mice and Men*. It may not be Shakespeare, but those writers sure tried.
- "Toni's Boys": In a story taken almost directly from Edgar Allan Poe's "The Cask of Amontillado," Kelly, Kris, and Tiffany find themselves tied together as they are being entombed alive in a wine cellar. It was not a very good wine year!
- "To See an Angel Die": Kris and her fellow Angels are flying to Hawaii to work out of the office there. But before she can buy some champagne to celebrate, Kris finds herself kidnapped and taken for a long ride in the back of a truck. Thank goodness for the

1,001 uses of rock salt—the salt you save may be your own!

- "Waikiki Angels": As undercover lifeguards, Kris and Kelly are held captive by thugs and end up with their hands and feet bound. A smile can a long way, as does a hidden walkie-talkie, so even at the worst time possible, it's a good idea to keep the bad guys guessing at what you're up to.

Case Plot

A well-to-do widow has been mysteriously robbed. Believing that this is an inside job, Sabrina becomes her assistant, while Kelly and Jill seek the assistance of Madame Dorian, a financial advisor who can communicate with the dead. Kelly is unknowingly hypnotized by Madame Dorian's assistant, Terrance, and ends up exposing their covers. While she is under his spell, he forces Kelly to take Jill on a dangerous car ride that almost kills them both. After breaking the trance, Jill and Kelly speed off to the client's house and meet up with Terrance as he's in the midst of stealing from their client for one last time.

Gayest Moment

When Kelly is hypnotized during the séance, she begins to babble about her doll Lillibet and the evil matron Beamish. In flashbacks, the scene of a very young Kelly being locked into the closet is so *Mommy Dearest! We love it!!!*

Mega-famous Star Alert

Actor René Auberjonois guest-stars in the episode as Madame Dorian's assistant, Terrance, and is the brains behind the hypnotic robberies. Auberjonois is best known for his roles in *Benson, Star Trek: Deep Space Nine,* and *Boston Legal.*

Comments

This episode has become a cult classic with fans. You get to see, via flashbacks, Kelly as a child as she is being abused by Beamish, the matron in the orphanage she grew up in. Fans have always wanted to know who played Beamish. Unfortunately, that actress is uncredited.

Episode #12: "Angels on Wheels"

Written by: Charles Sailor, Jack. V. Fogarty, and Rick Husky
Story by: Charles Sailor
Director: Richard Benedict
Airdate: December 22, 1976

Case Plot

Karen Jason, a roller derby skater, is deliberately murdered. Jill poses as the dead woman's sister Barbara, and becomes the newest member of the roller derby team. Sabrina chimes in as an investigator for the State Board of Insurance, while Kelly becomes a reporter for *Women's View* magazine.

The case speeds up when Kelly's car explodes just after she uncovers a suitcase full of money and fake driver's licenses. As she makes a deal to return the licenses, she finds out that Jill's cover has been blown and she's slated to be the next "accident." Kelly, Boz, and Sabrina race against time to save Jill . . . but it's Jill who decides to turn the tables and make co-conspirator Bad Betty regret the day she was born.

Tidbits

Kelly is on the phone talking to Charlie, and he tells her that there is a bomb attached to her car. How does he know this? As she jumps out of the car and begins to run away, Charlie yells for her to go back and get the suitcase. She runs back and grabs the suitcase, and just as she's out of harm's way, the car explodes.

Gayest Moment

"Stud of the Month" Red Loomis (Steve Sandor) showcases his oiled-up bare chest and proves that he has what it takes to "hold that pose" and be the next centerfold of the month.

Episode #16: "Dirty Business"

Written by: Edward J. Lasko
Director: Bill Bixby
Airdate: February 2, 1977

Case Plot

The Angels are hired to find out why someone tried to burn down a film lab. When interviewing investors, Bosley and Sabrina discover that the lab is a front for a porn studio. The Angels begin screening the "free-form" films and uncover that one of the movies inadvertently contains footage of a dirty cop fleeing from a scene after planting evidence.

Tidbit

This episode aired on Farrah Fawcett's thirtieth birthday.

Gayest Moment

When Sabrina, Jill, and Kelly are taking a break after watching hours of very dull film, they see an ultra-sexy and mature "Little Bo Peep" walk by. Soon after, a strapping "Shepherd Boy" walks by with his sheep. He's one fine shepherd! Oh, Bo-Peep!!

Famous Director

This episode was directed by actor Bill Bixby, who was best known as Dr. David Bruce Banner in the 1970s TV series *The Incredible Hulk*.

Episode #19: "Dancing in the Dark"

Written by: Les Carter
Director: Cliff Bole
Airdate: February 23, 1977

Case Plot

The widow of a legendary baseball player is being blackmailed with compromising photos after going out on a date with her dance instructor. Jill gets hired on at the dance studio, while Sabrina sets herself up as a mentally challenged woman and the next blackmail victim. Kelly becomes thick as thieves with the blackmailers and agrees to photograph the next incident. After her cover is blown, Kelly is held captive in a bowling alley until Jill and Sabrina are able to rescue her.

Gayest Moment

Sabrina acts drunk while Tony (Dennis Cole) tries to undress her and Kelly takes photos of the filthy event. Now that sounds like a fun threesome!

Celestial Hunk Alert

Actor Dennis Cole guest-stars as Tony Bordinay, the sexy and very smooth dance instructor who gets the women into compromising positions as they are being photographed. Off camera, Cole became romantically linked with Angel Jaclyn Smith during this episode, and they were married briefly from 1978 to 1981. Cole also appeared in two more episodes, "Unidentified Flying Angels" (episode #29) and "Terror on Skis" (episode #62).

Episode #21: "Angels at Sea"

Written by: John D.F. Black
Director: Allen Baron
Airdate: March 23, 1977

Case Plot

The Angels take on the case of a luxury cruise line that has had a string of accidents. Sabrina, Jill, Kelly, and Bosley sail into some dangerous waters because the killer already knows who they are even before they set foot on the ship. After Kelly fakes her own death, the Angels are able to flush out the man behind the accidents. However, it's only the tip of the iceberg after they find out that he has set three bombs to explode. So the Angels set out to defuse the bombs before they all go *Boom!*

Tidbit

This episode was filmed on the *Queen Mary,* which is docked in Long Beach, California. The *Queen Mary* was the sister ship to the *Queen Elizabeth,* both of which served as troop ships during WWII.

Gayest Moments

Good old dependable Bosley is hit on the head and stripped naked and is later found walking around the upper deck wearing nothing but a life preserver. Thank goodness it wasn't a bikini!

Mega-famous Star Alert

Actor Frank Gorshin plays Harry Dana, the man behind the accidents on the ship. Gorshin was considered to be one of the greatest impressionists in show business. He is best known for his work as the Riddler on the 1960s TV series *Batman,* for which he earned an Emmy nomination.

Lost Angel Episode: "Las Vegas Twist"

Written by: Ben Masselink

Second Draft: July 27, 1976

This episode was never produced. The case has a former client of Charlie's hiring the Angels to find his granddaughter, who has been kidnapped by her biological mother. The Angels track the case to Las Vegas, where the trail turns into a million-dollar robbery.

Tidbit

One particular scene has Kelly playing a cocktail waitress. She is given a room key by a patron. After another guy hits on her, she gives him the first man's room key and tells him to meet her there. Does this sound familiar? A similar scene was filmed for the episode *Lady Killer.* Instead of Kelly, it was Jill who was the cocktail waitress.

Episode #22: "The Blue Angels"

Written by: Edward J. Lasko
Story by : Laurie Lasko
Director: Georg Stanford Brown
Airdate: May 4, 1977

Case Plot

After two deaths at Paradise Massage, the Angels believe that someone on the police force is on the take. Kelly returns to the police academy as a cadet, Sabrina transfers into the local police precinct, and Jill and Bosley re-open Paradise Massage, setting in motion a sting to nab all the dirty cops. But halfway through the case, Sabrina's ex-husband unknowingly exposes all their covers. As they are all taken to a nearby automobile wrecking yard, the Angels are forced to contend with meeting their maker.

Gayest Moment

Breshnick, the owner of the massage parlor, does not like to be touched and preaches that everyone should only wear leaves, not clothing.

Semi-Angel-Regular
Michael Bell plays Sabrina's ex-husband Bill Duncan. Bill was also seen in "Target: Angels" (episode #5).

Cherub Guest Star Alert
Joanna Kerns plays Natalie Sands, the prostitute who is almost killed twice in this episode. Kerns went on to play Maggie Malone Seaver in the hit 1980s family show *Growing Pains.* And in 1993, she teamed up with future Angel, Shelley Hack, for the TV movie *Not in My Family,* in which they play sisters who are survivors of incest from the man they trusted the most, their father.

Celestial Hunk Alert
Dirk Benedict plays Barton, one of the young cadets on the take. He also appeared in "The Jade Trap" (episode #44). Benedict is best known for his role as sexy Lt. Starbuck on the 1970s series *Battlestar Galactica.* Later, in the 1980s, he was part of *The A-Team* as Lt. Templeton "Faceman" Peck. And in 1987, Benedict went on to play a con man who falls for future Angel, Tanya Roberts, in the wrestling movie *Body Slam.*

Season Two

Episode #23: "Angels in Paradise" (two-hour episode)
Written by: John D.F. Black
Director: Charles S. Dubin
Airdate: September 14, 1977

The Case File Breakdowns: Season Two, 1977–1978

Angels	*Airtime*	*Final Rating*	*Cost per Episode*
Sabrina Duncan Kelly Garrett Kris Munroe John Bosley	Wednesday 9 p.m.– 10 p.m. EST/PST	4	$390,000

Case Plot

After Jill leaves the agency, she is replaced by her kid sister Kris Munroe. No sooner does Kris walk into the office than they find out that Charlie has been kidnapped and they dash off to Hawaii to find him. They soon find themselves breaking a convict out of prison to exchange for Charlie. But before they can make the trade, Charlie is taken by force from his captors. The Angels then devise an elaborate plan to rescue Charlie and have his second set of captors framed for harboring the fugitive that they broke out of jail. In the end, Charlie escapes before the Angels get to see him. Aloha, Angels!

Tidbit

This was the first episode featuring new Angel, Kris Munroe. Jill thought Kris was going to college, but she was actually attending the San Francisco Police Academy. No wonder we like her!

Gayest Moment

Kris finds herself with "no cover" on a nude beach, trying to talk with a contact. Thank goodness she did find a palm branch; otherwise many boys would have gone blind. And hopefully she packed some sunscreen.

Mega-famous Star Alert

Entertainer Don Ho is a close friend of Charlie's that Sabrina contacts to get additional information on his captors. Ho was best known for his signature song, "Tiny Bubbles" and was a native of Hawaii. Don Ho does sing in the original airing of the show, but that scene was edited out when the episode was broken into two one-hour episodes for syndication. This same edited version is also on the 2005 DVD release.

Angel Memory: Cheryl Ladd

On wearing her first bikini: "I was most famous for the one I wore climbing onto the boat in 'Angels in Paradise.' I was one of the first women to wear a Brazilian high-cut bikini like that on television."

Gay Character Alert—Episode #24: "Angels on Ice" (two-hour episode)

Written by: Rick Edelstein
Director: Robert Kelljan
Airdate: September 21, 1977

Case Plot

The Angels investigate an ice show after the lead skaters mysteriously disappear. Kelly and Kris con their way into becoming skaters, while Bosley and Sabrina sell concessions. After following one of the suspects, Kelly is kidnapped, leaving the Angels to figure out what happened to her. She eventually escapes and rushes back to the ice show, just as they begin to perform on opening night. In the end, Kris puts all the clues together and

Kate Jackson in Hawaii, coming back from the set of filming the season two premiere "Angels in Paradise." (© Cynthia A. Lai)

saves the lives of the visiting diplomats who were the targets of assassins.

Gayest Moment

Alvin, chorographer of the ice capades, was one of the few gay characters seen on *Charlie's Angels.* He was always wearing outrageous colored outfits and smelling like *Canoe* cologne. (Note: Canoe is a real cologne that has a refined, spicy, lavender, amber smell. It was created way back in 1932 and is still available today.)

Mega-famous Stars Alert

Phil Silvers, the legendary comedian-actor, finds himself in the midst of Angels as the owner of the ice show. He is best known for his TV show, *The Phil Silvers Show,* for which he won an Emmy. He also won two Tony Awards for *Top Banana* and a revival of *A Funny Thing Happened on the Way to the Forum.* His daughter Cathy Silvers played Jenny Piccalo on *Happy Days.*

Comic actor Jim Backus played Iggy, the ice show prop man who is kidnapped and helps Kelly escape to save the day. Backus is best known for his role as Thurston Howell III on *Gilligan's Island.* He is also immortalized as the character "Mr. Magoo" in the cartoon series.

Episode #25: "Pretty Angels All in a Row"

Written by: John D.F. Black
Director: John D.F. Black
Airdate: September 28, 1977

The smart Angel, Kate Jackson, in Hawaii during the filming of "Angels in Paradise." (© Cynthia A. Lai)

Case Plot

The Miss Chrysanthemum Pageant contestants are being scared off. Kelly and Kris sign on as beauty contestants, while Sabrina and Bosley play a reporter and cameraman covering the event. Just as one of the judges goes missing, Kris finds herself being shot at. When Sabrina goes to check out the replacement judge at the airport, she finds two men handing her bridge money. Sabrina decides to hitch a ride with the two men in the back of their car trunk, but she is eventually found, and they kidnap her. While tied up, Sabrina discovers that a contestant's father is swaying the judges so that his daughter wins.

Gayest Moment

The Miss Chrysanthemum song itself. It's so memorable! Surely it's running through your head right now! "Hi there! Hello . . ." Someday iTunes will have it for sale.

Angel Memory: Jaclyn Smith

"I had injured myself while dancing. I hadn't warmed up properly and we were rushing to film. That was kind of crazy."

Episode #27: "Circus of Terror"

Written by: Robert Janes
Director: Allen Baron
Airdate: October 19, 1977

Case Plot

The Barzak Circus may have to close its doors after a string of serious mishaps, and the Angels are brought in by the owner's son to investigate. Sabrina takes on the role of a mime apprentice, Kelly jumps over things with her motorcycle as "Go-Go Garrett," and Kris is a showgirl who assists the knife thrower. Things heat up under the big top as Kris and Kelly almost get burned alive in their tent, while Sabrina finds a snake in her bed. Eventually they discover that all the accidents are being caused by one of the performers, who blames the Barzaks for the death of his niece.

Clothing

Feel like you're having déjà vu? Does that red-sequined outfit that Kris is wearing seem very familiar? It should.

Her sister Jill was caught wearing exactly the same outfit when she was prancing around as a "Feline" in "Lady Killer." Nice to know that these sisters liked to share everything!

Gayest Moment

A little woman named, Tinkle Belle has the hots for Bosley. She follows him around the circus as if he were prime meat at a fat farm. Yes, Bosley, John Bosley . . . don't forget about Tinkle Belle!!! Oh, yeah, *baby*!

Comments

This is the very first episode Cheryl Ladd filmed for the series. It was her screen test for ABC executives. After they saw her work, she was made the new Angel! The first day on the set, Ladd wore a shirt that said, "Farrah Fawcett–Minor."

Angel Memory: Cheryl Ladd

"Obviously there weren't really knives being thrown at me. They popped out from behind the board. But it was dangerous. When I was standing, I could not move a muscle because they were *fired* out the back like a gunshot. If I had moved while they were firing, it wouldn't have been pretty. It was a little nerve-racking."

Episode #31: "Angel Baby"

Written by: George R. Hodges and John D.F. Black
Story by: George R. Hodges
Director: Paul Stanley
Airdate: November 16, 1977

Case Plot

A friend from Kelly's past asks her for help after he is arrested for causing a disturbance while looking for his girlfriend. After questioning the missing girl's roommates, Kelly finds out that girl was expecting and planning to sell her baby to a black market baby agency. Kelly poses as an expectant mother, while Kris crashes a party looking for lonely men to find some fast cash, leaving Sabrina and Bosley on the market looking for a baby to adopt. After Kelly's cover is blown, she is forced to deliver the missing girl's baby. As they are about to be killed, Bosley, Sabrina, and Kris come to their rescue.

Tidbit

This is a very emotional episode for rookie Angel Kris, as she shoots and kills her very first criminal. Sabrina comforts her through this difficult moment. It's such an Angel-luscious tearjerker moment.

Gayest Moments

Kris goes to a hotel room to have sex and produce a child. The guy is cute, but apparently the only *big* thing he has is his conscience. Who wouldn't want to jump into the sack with Kris?

Angel Memory: Cheryl Ladd

"It was a big dramatic moment for my character and showed a side of funny little Kris that we had not seen before."

Angel Memory: Cheryl Ladd

On shooting a gun: "I went between two sound stages with the props guy. He showed me how to hold it properly. Eventually he said, 'That was really good, honey, but can you do it with your eyes open?' Every time I pulled the trigger, I would close my eyes. It's kind of important to look at what you're aiming at."

Episode #32: "Angels in the Wings"

Written by: Edward J. Lasko
Director: Dennis Donnelly
Airdate: November 23, 1977

Case Plot

A new film version of the musical *Sweet Misery* has stopped production after a few accidents have threatened the safety of the cast and crew. The Angels go to Hollywood as Kris is given the sexy young lead in the movie. When the filming resumes, a stage light nearly hits Kris. As they continue to investigate the jinxed set theory, they watch old film footage of an actress falling to her death with a mute stagehand rushing to her side. In a background check, the Angels discover that the stagehand lives near the soundstage. Kelly and Kris re-create the events that led to the actress's accident to force him out of hiding.

Gayest Moment

What is not to love about this episode? It's one big musical! Plus we get to see Cheryl Ladd showcasing her singing and dancing talents. Now, besides the hair, the makeup, and clothes, they're singing and dancing. Does it get any gayer than this?

Mega-famous Stars Alert

Shari Wallis is best known for her role in the musical feature film *Oliver* (1968) as Nancy.

Gene Barry was nominated for a 1984 Tony Award as Best Actor (Musical) for *La Cage aux Folles.* In 1994, future Angel Tanya Roberts appeared in Barry's TV series, *Burke's Law,* in the episode "Who Killed Nick Hazard?" Roberts plays detective Julie Reardon, one of the main suspects at a detective convention in which a fellow detective is mysteriously murdered.

Tidbits

Soundstage 8 was used as a backdrop in this episode. This same soundstage contained the interior sets where *Charlie's Angels* was filmed.

This was also the very first episode in which Cheryl Ladd showed off her singing talent.

Angel Memory: Cheryl Ladd

"I loved it. It was really fun to use those skills."

Episode #33: "Magic Fire"

Written by: Lee Sheldon
Director: Leon Carrere
Airdate: November 30, 1977

Case Plot

A magician known as the Magic Man is believed to be responsible for the rash of fires at Fashion City warehouses. The main suspect hires the Angels to find out who's framing him. The team materializes at the Magic

"Albert was beautiful, again another professional. Everything I told him he did. If I told him to sit in the motor home, he would sit in the motor home. If I told him to sit in the booth and eat food, he did. He was just adorable."

—Jaclyn Smith, on acting with her poodle named Albert. Albert acted in four episodes, including "Magic Fire."

Castle, with Bosley and Kris posing as a magician and his assistant and Kelly as a famous magician's daughter with secrets to sell. And Sabrina infiltrates Fashion City as a designer from Paris.

After escaping a warehouse fire, Sabrina later goes back and discovers that the phone inside was rigged to start the fire. Upon closer scrutiny, Sabrina finds another phone ready to ignite more destruction. As Kris waits backstage, she catches a magician's assistant placing a short call and hanging up. The phone rings back, and Kris confirms to Sabrina that the arsonist is the magician's assistant.

Tidbits

Prince Charles dropped by the set during production of this episode. Much of the filming was done on location at the Magic Castle in Hollywood, California, and Jaclyn Smith's poodle, Albert, made his third guest appearance.

Gayest Moment

Kate Jackson's character, Maxine Myntie, has an over-the-top French accent and a white French poodle by her side. It's priceless!

Missing Charlie

During the magic show, Charlie is actually in the audience and hands Kris his pen. Unfortunately, Kris does not remember what he looks like. I guess the great Zolton erased her memory!

Angel Memory: Leonard Goldberg

"During the production of the series, Prince Charles was visiting America and came to Los Angeles. Twentieth Century Fox had a huge luncheon for him at the studio. At the time he was one of the world's most eligible bachelors. During the lunch, one of his assistants came over to me and said, 'The Prince would like to know why the Angels aren't here.' I explained to him that we were behind in our production schedule and that they were shooting right through lunch. I watched as he went back and whispered to the Prince. A few minutes later dessert was served, and Prince Charles took a polite bite and then stood up. Immediately, as decorum dictated, several hundred people at the luncheon also stood up. His assistant came back over to me and said, 'His Highness would like to visit the set.' I then proceeded to lead Prince Charles, his entourage, and about sixty members of the international press across the lot to the *Charlie's Angels* stage. I introduced Prince Charles to the Angels, and he was extremely charming. He then stepped outside the stage door and posed with the Angels for the swarm of photographers and said, 'Now you know why they are called Charlie's Angels.' The flashbulbs exploded, and in the next day or two, the photograph was seen around the world."

Episode #34: "Sammy Davis Jr. Kidnap Caper"

Written by: Ron Friedman
Director: Ronald Austin
Airdate: December 7, 1977

Case Plot

The Angels are hired on as bodyguards for Sammy Davis Jr. after a foiled kidnapping attempt. After several more tries, Sammy's look-alike, Herbie Brubaker III, is taken by mistake and held for ransom. Due to the odd amount requested, the Angels begin reviewing financial records of all of Davis's employees and narrow it down to one. Unknowingly, he leads the Angels and Sammy to where Herbie is being held, and they rescue him from his captors.

Gayest Moment

Georgie (Martin Kove), one of the bad guys who kidnaps Herbie, is constantly shirtless and showing off his sexy hairy chest all throughout the episode.

Clues

Character actor Norman Alden, who plays bad guy Louis Fluellen, was a close friend of Sammy Davis Jr. Davis always had Alden play "the heavy" in his films because he trusted him with the rough scenes. Alden also appeared in "Dancin' Angels" (episode #86) and "Taxi Angels" (episode #102).

Mega-Super Guest Star

Sammy Davis Jr. played two roles in this episode, himself and Herbie Brubaker III, a Sammy Davis Jr. impersonator. Davis was a member of the Rat Pack. He was nominated for a Tony Award for the 1964 musical *Golden Boy.* And in 1981, he worked with Angel Farrah Fawcett in the comedy film *The Cannonball Run.*

Angel Memory: Jaclyn Smith

"Sammy was great!"

Angel Memory: Cheryl Ladd

"Sammy Davis Jr. was a hoot! We had a ball with him. He was fun, fun, fun and really nice to all of us."

WARNING: Most Annoying Charlie's Angels *Episode—Episode #41: "Angel Blues"*

Written by: Edward J. Lakso
Director: Georg Stanford Brown
Airdate: February 8, 1978

Case Plot

Charlie's favorite country singer has a nervous breakdown. After a long taxi ride, she is dropped off at her father's and is greeted by two thugs who give her an overdose of heroin. What makes this the most annoying episode is listening to this one-hit-wonder's song, "Trippin' to the Mornin" being played over and over and over again. By the time you finish the episode, you will have wished that the thugs at the beginning of the episode could have given you an overdose at the same time.

Tidbit

The song was sung by Lynne Marta, who also played Linda in "One Love . . . Two Angels" (episodes #92–93).

Episode #42: "Mother Goose Is Running for His Life"

Written by: Del Reisman, Ronald Austin, and James Buchanan
Director: George McCowan
Airdate: February 15, 1978

Case Plot

After some odd mishaps at Mother Goose Toys, the owner believes that someone is trying to force him to

FLAWLESS MAKEUP

- "To Kill an Angel": Kelly Garrett is lying in the hospital bed after being shot in the head. Her angelic face is so heavenly, the only way one would know she has been shot in the head would be the gauze strip on her forehead.
- "Diamond in the Rough": After a hard day's work with a wealthy auto mechanic, Kris might have a few oil smudges on her heavenly face, but she still looks picture-perfect. Even hard labor does not keep a Angel down.
- "Hours of Desperation": Even though she might go "Boom-Boom," sexy Sabrina looks radiant after she jumps in the lake while held hostage with a not-so-fashionable belt around her waist made of dynamite.
- "Angel Hunt": Kelly, Tiffany, and Kris are trapped on a deserted island without their purses! Even after a couple of days, their hair and makeup were still perfect. Maybe there was a Sephora store on the island!
- "Hula Angels": Captured and put into in a cage, Julie is on cloud nine with her sexy, perfect makeup and hair. Maybe it was all her female captors who kept her appearance so on-target.
- "Let Our Angel Live": Poor Kelly was shot in the head again!! In the final episode of the series, she had flawless makeup all throughout the surgery and recovery. Even with her head bandages, she looked flawless.

sell his toy company. He brings in the Angels to investigate. Sabrina comes in as a new toy consultant from Hong Kong, Kelly gets hired on as a professional wiretap, and Kris poses as a model. After the mysterious death of a burglar who broke into the factory, they learn that all the occurrences were caused by a disgruntled employee who wanted the owner dead.

Tidbit

This episode does a shameless promotion of the *Charlie's Angels'* dolls at the end of the episode. Too bad it aired almost two months after Christmas!

After being given the "Kelly Garrett doll," Kelly mentions that she wants one for her niece. Did she forget that she was an orphan? Maybe it was the massive gunshot wound from season one that made her forget?

Angel Memory: Cheryl Ladd

"I loved playing the rag doll. I had more fun with that. I loved all the goofy characters I got to play and the fun things I got to create. In those areas it gave us an opportunity for each of us at certain times to create little fun moments. I loved being that life-sized doll. I didn't have to look sexy with my perfect hair."

Episode #43: "Little Angels of the Night"

Written by: Mickey Rose
Director: Georg Stanford Brown
Airdate: February 22, 1978

Case Plot

After an attack on a call girl, Dolly Smith, a very dear old, old friend of Charlie's (very old) hires the Angels.

The Angels become the newest additions to Dolly's apartment building, where the tenants are female prostitutes. After a few more attacks, a pattern emerges that the attacker is focusing on only blondes. The Angels tag the pizza delivery man as the attacker, but Kris realizes it's the restaurant owner when he chooses to make her his next victim.

Gayest Moment

The Angels plus Bosley on bikes in a high-speed chase. Thank goodness they were able to pedal super-fast to catch the bad guy.

Missing Charlie

Even after the Angels become three of Dolly's newest "working girls," she doesn't divulge to them what Charlie looks like.

Gay Character Alert—Episode #45: "Angels on the Run"

Actor Sy Kramer plays the gay dress shop owner Roger. He meets Kris at Rosie's coffee shop, gives her some fashion advice (as if she needs it), and points out that he saw the robbers throwing a package into the back of the missing truck driver's vehicle.

Season Three

Episode #47: "Angels in Vegas" (two hours)

Written by: Edward J. Lakso
Director: Robert Kelljan
Airdate: September 13, 1978

The Case File Breakdowns: Season Three, 1978–1979

Angels	*Airtime*	*Final Rating*	*Cost per Episode*
Sabrina Duncan Kelly Garrett Kris Munroe John Bosley Jill Munroe (3 cases)	Wednesday, 9 p.m.–10 p.m. EST/PST	12	$440,000

Case Plot

After the mysterious death of a showgirl, the Angels are hired by casino owner Frank Howell, who feels someone is trying to gaslight him. Kelly becomes a cancan dancer, while Kris performs as a lounge singer with her idol Marty Cole, leaving Sabrina to flirt with the client. After an attempt on Sabrina's life and the death of his best friend, Howell dismisses the Angels. But before they can leave, Kris gets kidnapped, and it's revealed that Marty is behind all the crimes and blames Frank for the death of his wife.

Hair Alert

This is a very important footnote. Sabrina changed her hairstyle in this episode. It's fuller, fluffier, and sexier! Unfortunately, it only lasts for this one episode—then she goes back to her chic straight look.

Tidbits

Spelling and Goldberg cross-promoted their new TV series *Vega$* by having Bosley arrange a meeting be-

The full cast of *Charlie's Angels:* David Doyle, Kate Jackson, Jaclyn Smith, and Cheryl Ladd as they float into their third season. (© American Broadcasting Companies, Inc.)

tween private investigator Dan Tanna (Robert Urich) and the Angels. *Vega$* premiered just after this episode.

And Robert Urich worked again with Cheryl Ladd when they played husband and wife in the controversial

1979 TV movie *When She Was Bad,* in which Ladd played a child abuser. That episode led to Ladd's campaign to prevent child abuse and her becoming an Ambassador for Childhelp USA.

Gayest Moment

Kris and Kelly feel the flame of desire when they finally meet sexy Dan Tanna (Robert Urich) at the tail end of this episode. Bosley kept trying to get them to meet Dan throughout the episode. Their eyes went ga-ga over Dan!

Alley Cat Alert

While auditioning for a part in a Vegas show, Kelly pulls out a chair to stop her competition from auditioning before she gets the chance. As her rival falls to the ground, Kelly dances her way into the job.

Mega-famous Star Alert

Entertainer Dean Martin costarred in this episode as Frank Howell, the owner of the casino. Martin was one of the original Rat Pack and performed on TV, film, and stage. He had his own TV show, *The Dean Martin Show,* for which he won a Golden Globe and was given two stars on the Walk of Fame in Hollywood.

Dick Sargent plays the evil Marty Cole, who sets out to destroy Frank Howell and his casino empire. Sargent was best known for his work in *Bewitched.* Later in life he came out about being gay and was an advocate for gay rights.

Angel Memory: Cheryl Ladd
"Dean Martin was handsome and charming."

Episode #48: "Angel Come Home"

Written by: Stephen Kandel
Director: Paul Stanley
Airdate: September 20, 1978

Case Plot
Jill returns home after receiving a frantic telegraph from Kris. It turns out to be from Paul Ferrino, a fellow race-car drive who wants Jill to race and protect his new high-tech racecar. After someone tries to blow up the car, Jill's fiancé arrives and is very suspicious. He eventually takes the car for a spin around the track, and it explodes. Jill realizes that the car was a fraud and the explosion was meant to kill her.

Tidbit
Farrah Fawcett returns to the series in this first of six guest appearances.

Gayest Moment
All throughout the episode, Jill's hairstyle and clothes are constantly changing. She looks just *heavenly*!

Clothing
Check out Kris's shoes in the opening scene. When she's walking into her beach house, she is wearing high heels. As she runs out the door and onto the beach, they miraculously turn into a pair of flats. Now that's talent!

Celestial Hunk Alert

Stephen Collins plays Steve Carmody, who is engaged to Jill. Their love affair ran short after he was killed off in a car explosion. Collins later went on to play Reverend Eric Camden in Aaron Spelling's long-running TV series, *7th Heaven.*

Episode #50: "Angels in Springtime"

Written by: William Froug
Director: Larry Stewart
Airdate: October 10, 1978

Case Plot

Actors to the stage . . . but not after the great Eve Le Deux, Broadway actress, has been murdered at the Springtime Spa. Charlie sends the Angels to find out why. Sabrina becomes Springtime's newest dietitian, Kris is the newest exercise instructor, and Kelly takes the high road as a wealthy guest. The Angels find out that the workers at the spa are blackmailing their guests, that Le Deux's death was due to a tell-all book she was writing, and that her best friend Norma killed her for it.

Tidbit

Not many episodes had references to past cases. Kelly mentions she can no longer be hypnotized. She was hypnotized in "The Séance," (episode 11) and after that learned how not to be affected by hypnotism. So when the overtly lesbian doctor tries to put her under, Kelly fakes it.

And Mercedes McCambridge, who played Eve Le

Deux's best friend Norma, was the possessed voice of Linda Blair in the movie *The Exorcist.*

Gayest Moment

Kris is almost killed from being smothered with hot steaming towels by the vastly overweight Zora. And the female doctor tries to put the lesbian moves on Kelly by pre-warming the stethoscope before placing it on her. It's getting really *hot* in here, ladies!!

Missing Charlie

Eve Le Deux's niece shows the Angels a photo of Charlie and Eve when they performed in *A Midsummer Night's Dream* together. But Charlie was disguised as a jackass.

Episode #51: "Winning Is for Losers"

Written by: Ray Brenner
Director: Cliff Bole
Airdate: October 18, 1978

Case Plot

Kris's best friend, a famous female golfer, has been receiving threats to leave the tournament. Kris asks her fellow Angels to help her uncover who is behind the threats. The Angels take on the task of guarding Linda throughout the golf tournament. They discover that her manager is behind the threats.

Tidbit

The episode centered around golf. Cheryl Ladd eventually became an avid golfer and in 2005 published the book *Token Chick,* on her tips about and memories of the game. Ladd also has had her own PRO-AM golf tournament.

Gayest Moment

After a crossing bridge collapses, Kris gets down and dirty with an alligator! Super Angel scary!

Cherub Guest Star Alert

Jamie Lee Curtis plays Lynda Frye, a pro golfer who is best friends with Kris. Curtis went on to become the 1970s and 1980s scream queen in such hits as *Halloween, Halloween 2, Prom Night, Terror Train,* and *The Fog.* Her success continued into the 1990s with *True Lies,* for which she won a Golden Globe. She also keeps busy with her work with the Starlight Foundation.

Mega-famous Star Alert

Casey Kasem plays reporter Tom Rogers. Kasem is well known as the voice of "Shaggy" for the Scooby-Doo cartoon. He is also known for doing the American Top 40 Countdown for over twenty years and as the voice of Alexander Cabot III in *Josie and the Pussycats* with Ladd

Prior to filming this episode, both Kasem and Jaclyn Smith had guest-starred in the Hardy Boys/Nancy Drew Mysteries episode "Mystery of the Hollywood Phantom," in which Smith plants a big wet kiss onto Hardy Boy Parker Stevenson after mistaking him for an extra on the set of *Charlie's Angels.*

ATTACK ANIMALS

The Angels had to go up against some evil bad guys, but they also had to go up against some pretty nasty animals too. Here is a list of animals that wanted to make a heavenly supper out of an Angel:

- "Circus of Terror": Sabrina finds she has an unwanted guest in her bed—a snake. No matter how much he tries to charm her with his rattles, she just wasn't entranced by him.
- "Winning Is for Losers": Kris might have met her match when she has to wrestle an alligator. But if she's determined to turn him into a purse and a pair of matching shoes, there might still be hope!
- "Angel Hunt": Tiffany awakes from her fall into the river and finds herself face-to-face with a tiger. Afraid of becoming his dinner, Tiff uses her heavenly voice and instructs the tiger to stay in his own space. He's one smart tiger if he knows the deeper meaning of EST.

"I loved David Doyle, like crazy."

—Cheryl Ladd

Episode #53: "Pom Pom Angels"

Written by: Richard Carr
Director: Cliff Bole
Airdate: November 1, 1978

Case Plot

Holy long hair! Sexy cheerleaders keep disappearing one by one. After each incident, religious messages start appearing. Kris and Kelly pull out their pom-poms to find out why. Kris is drugged and kidnapped by a religious freak and is forced to be a part of "The Good One's" cult. But before she can turn from her evil ways, the Angels takes down the Good One and free the cheerleaders.

Gayest Moment

The Angels try to sell themselves as models to go on a boat cruise. But in the end, it's really Charlie offering them a well-deserved vacation!

Alley Cat Alert

When Margo tries to cut Kris's beautiful blonde Angel hair, the devil emerges from this Angel and stops her. Nothing like kicking some cult ass!

Cherub Guest Star Alert

Anne Francis plays cult member Margo, who worships the "Good One" and tries to give Kris a haircut. She also guest-starred in "Angels of the Deep" (episode #96). Francis is best known for her Emma Peel–type role in Aaron Spelling's series *Honey West,* for which she won a Golden Globe. She also appeared opposite Barbara

Streisand in *Funny Girl* and received a Hollywood Walk of Fame star for her work in television.

Cherub Guest Star Alert—Episode #56: Jordan Ladd in "Angel on My Mind"

Airdate: November 22, 1978

Cheryl Ladd's real-life daughter Jordan portrays Kris as a child in one of the flashback scenes. Jordan has grown up to be one of today's hottest up-and-coming talents. She has worked in such feature films as *Grindhouse, Cabin Fever,* and *Hostel: Part II.* And in 1998, Cheryl and Jordan played mother and daughter in the thriller *Every Mother's Worst Fear.*

Episode #60: "Counterfeit Angels"

Written by: Richard Carr
Director: Georg Stanford Brown
Airdate: January 24, 1979

Case Plot

There is double trouble in Los Angeles, with a second set of Angels on the prowl, but these Angels are counterfeits in disguise. Pretending to be the real Angels, they are robbing area businesses blind. Not taking this sitting down, Sabrina, Kelly, and Kris flee the police and begin investigating. After one of the imposters is injured, Sabrina steps into her role on the team. Soon after, the other two fake Angels are arrested, and Kelly and Kris assume their identities. Now the real Angels, disguised as themselves, are set to draw out everyone behind this scam and clear their names.

Tidbit
One of the best episodes of the season, it allows the Angels to poke fun at their characters and the show.

Gayest Moment
Kris watches a TV commercial of the fake Kris romping around and being seductive in a mattress garden. Those are some very happy mattresses.

Episode #64: "Teen Angels"

Written by: Bob Mitchell and Ester Mitchell
Story by: Laurie Lakso
Director: Allen Baron
Airdate: February 28, 1979

Case Plot
After a girl is murdered on an exclusive all-girl campus, the Angels go back to school to find out what really happened. Sabrina and Kelly join the teaching staff as the new art and English teachers, while Kris enrolls as a new student at the school. After one of the students, Donna, takes an instant dislike to Kris, it doesn't take long for them to uncover that she's selling pills and alcohol on campus. The Angels find out just how evil Donna is as she traps them in the barn and sets it on fire. Donna's friends turn on her, forcing Donna to reveal that it's the ranchhand who is the killer and he's set to make Kelly his next victim.

Gayest Moment
Donna twists Kris's hair just before she tries to yank the strands out of her head. Not very heavenly!

Angel Shelley Hack on the set on "Angel Hunt" during season four. (©catrescue@monmouth.com/Nancy Barr-Brandon)

Cherub Guest Star Alert

Audrey Landers is Donna, the wickedly twisted schoolgirl who has absolutely no conscience. Landers went on to play Afton Cooper on *Dallas* for eight seasons and played Val Clarke in the movie version of *A Chorus Line,* in which she sang "Dance 10, Looks 3." Currently she is in the hit USA Networks show, *Burn Notice.*

Season Four

Episode #69: "Love Boat Angels"

Written by: Edward J. Lakso
Director: Allen Baron
Airdate: September 12, 1979

Case Plot

After millions of priceless art pieces go missing, the Angels are hired to retrieve evidence on the man who is thought to have stolen them. Kelly, Kris, Bosley, and the newest Angel, Tiffany Welles, all jump aboard *The Love Boat* and set sail to the Virgin Islands. En route, Kris

The Case File Breakdowns: Season Four, 1979–1980

Angels	*Airtime*	*Final Rating*	*Cost per Episode*
Kelly Garrett Kris Munroe Tiffany Welles John Bosley Jill Munroe (3 cases)	Wednesday 9 p.m.–10 p.m. EST/PST	20	$450,000

meets Paul Hollister, a modern-day Robin Hood. In St. Barts, things begin heat up as Kris begins to fall head over halo for Paul. As they begin to retrieve the stolen art pieces, peril ensues when Kelly and the client are kidnapped. In the end, the client buys back the missing art pieces, and Kris ends up with a broken heart when she has to say goodbye to her Robin Hood.

Case In-depth

This is the first case for Shelley Hack as Tiffany Welles. She replaced Kate Jackson in the series. Hack is a stunning beauty who was best known for her ads for Revlon's Charlie cologne. From the start, Hack brought her great sense of high fashion to the show with the help of designer Nolan Miller.

Gayest Moment

The cast of *The Love Boat* appeared in this episode, adding some lighthearted comedy with Doc, Gofer, and Isaac hitting on the Angels.

Spelling Connection

This episode had many of the hottest stars of the time, including Bert Convy, Bo Hopkins, Dick Sargent, and Judy Landers, along with *Love Boat* cast members Gavin MacLeod, Bernie Kopell, Fred Grandy, Ted Lange, and Lauren Tewes.

Missing Charlie

Tiffany Welles's father is a very old childhood friend of Charlie's. She even has the photo to prove it! Unfortunately, the photo was taken of Charlie as a child.

HEAVENLY COMIC RELIEF

Judy Landers created two unforgettable comedy roles on *Charlie's Angels.* In her first appearance, she was Mrs. Chicken ("Angels on the Run"), and in the second, Kris and Kelly thought she was Sabrina's replacement ("Love Boat Angels").

"I was still in high school at the time; nobody knew. It was so exciting because I had seen *Charlie's Angels* on television and said, 'I want to be on the TV one day.' I was lucky enough after auditioning for a few things to get that. I had always been a fan of Farrah, and I still am.

"*Charlie's Angels* was one of my first acting jobs I ever did. My scene as 'Mrs. Chicken' was all improvised. It was a great experience at the time. David Doyle was a great man. He loved to improvise, had a great sense of humor and was the containment professional. Unfortunately, I was not able to keep the 'Mrs. Chicken' hat. Although I wanted to, because it was one of the first times I ever was on television. So I really wanted to keep it, but they would not let me.

"Jaclyn Smith and Cheryl Ladd were great to work with. I remembered it was so amazing to me, since I was new to acting at the time and hadn't been on that many sets. I was shocked how many times they went into hair and makeup. I could not believe it; it was every ten minutes they would be back in the hair and makeup chair. They had the three chairs lined up. Each had her own hairdresser and makeup artist. I'm telling you the hair was back in rollers every ten minutes. I don't know how their hair withstood all that, but it did.

"I must say I did not get that special a treatment. It was almost like if one Angel went back for makeup, the others had to do it as well. It was like, 'She's touching up. I'd better touch up.' That was amazing to me, how much time they spent in the makeup chairs. They all are natural beauties; they all are just as beautiful if they didn't have a stitch of makeup on. But for the show to get that look they were always touching up and making the hair perfect and the makeup perfect.

"I remember my first day on the set, walking on. It was at 20th Century Fox, a rainy day at 5:30 in the morning. I arrive, perfectly on time. And there I saw Jaclyn Smith in her rollers and a big trench coat looking just beautiful without her makeup on. I thought, 'Wow they are amazing.'

"A little known fact was, I lost out for being the new Angel to Cheryl Ladd in 1977. I came down to the very end of it. I don't know, maybe I didn't have quite as much experience as her. I was very green, and people didn't know how old I was when I started my career. I was playing a Las Vegas showgirl and I was only seventeen years old when I was on *Vega$.*"

Awards
The Love Boat and *Charlie's Angels* won Most Amazing Cast Cross-Over Award at the 2003 TVLand award show. Cheryl Ladd accepted the award.

Tidbit
Judy Landers also worked with Jaclyn Smith and John Forsythe (Charlie) in the 1978 TV movie *The Users,* in which Smith a played an Arizona prostitute who works her way up the Hollywood ranks to become one of the most powerful women in Hollywood.

Episode #71: "Avenging Angel"

Written by: Edward J. Lakso
Story by Laurie Lasko
Director: Allen Baron
Airdate: September 26, 1979

"Jaclyn and I are still buddies. We were always good to each other, and we never fought. We always got along. She's a great girl."

—Cheryl Ladd

Cheryl Ladd taking a break during the filming of season four's "Angel Hunt. (©catrescue@monmouth.com/Nancy Barr-Brandon)

Case Plot

Frank Desmond, a junkie whom Kelly had sent to prison several years ago, has just been released from jail. Swearing revenge on Kelly, Frank sneaks into her home at night and injects her with heroin. Believing Kelly and Frank have their $2 million in drugs, the mob kidnaps them and injects them with more heroin. The mobsters wait for them to crash, but Kelly and Frank escape as Kris and Tiffany swoop in to save them from a pending death.

Gayest Moment

Kelly's hair! The more she gets hooked on heroin, the curlier her hair becomes. By the end of the episode, it's just *out of control.* This should have been the big tip-off for Kris and Tiffany. Evidently, crazy hair must be a side effect of doing smack. Just say no!

Celestial Hunk Alert

Steve Kanaly plays Harold Sims, one of the mob men who want the $2 million in heroin back from Frank. Kanaly is best known as Ray Krebbs from the hit CBS TV show *Dallas.*

Tidbits

Richard Bakalyan, who plays Eddie Feducci, costarred with Jaclyn Smith in the 1976 Disney TV movie, *The Whiz Kid and the Carnival Caper,* in which Bakalyan plays a robber plotting to break into a bank safe with the aid of one of its bank tellers (Smith).

Angel Memory: Jaclyn Smith

"That was one of my favorite shows, because it gave me a chance to go beyond the pretty Angel image and dirty up a bit, plus not do hair or makeup. It was a very emotional show for Kelly, and we all wanted our chance to break out. I loved it."

Mega-famous Star Alert—Episode #72: Kim Cattrall in "Angels at the Altar"

Airdate: October 3, 1979

Kim Cattrall plays Sharon Kellerman, a childhood friend of Kelly's who is about to get married. Sharon is worried someone is targeting her fiancé after a string of accidents. However, it's her fiancé who has devised an elaborate plan to kill her in order to inherit her vast wealth. Cattrall is known for the films *Star Trek VI: The Undiscovered Country* and *Masquerade,* but it was her role as sex-hungry Samantha Jones in HBO's *Sex and the City* that has made her a gay favorite!

Episode #73: "Fallen Angel"

Written by: Kathryn Michaelian Powers

Director: Allen Baron

Airdate: October 24, 1979

Case Plot

The Angels are hired to protect the Blue Heron Diamond from well-known diamond thief Damien Roth. But when Kelly follows Roth, she discovers that Jill Munroe is in Los Angeles and is dating Damien. When Kris confronts her sister about Damien, Jill demands that the Angels stop following her and Damien. Unknown to the Angels, Jill has been working undercover for Charlie to get close to him and become his accomplice. After Damien and Jill steal the diamond, Jill kicks his ass on the roof and arrests him.

Tidbit

This is the only episode in which one of the Angels went undercover without any of the others having knowledge of it. It was hot to see Jill turning bad! And it was not until *Charlie's Angels: Full Throttle* that we see another Angel gone bad, with Madison Lee, played convincingly by Demi Moore.

Alley Cat Alert

When Kelly confronts Jill about her budding romance with Damien, vicious words are exchanged, and these alley cats show their claws.

Celestial Hunk Alert

Timothy Dalton plays a 007-type jewel thief and Jill's love interest. How ironic that Dalton went on to play James Bond in *The Living Daylights* and *License to Kill.*

Another 007 connection is that future Angel Tanya Roberts played Stacey Sutton in 1985's *A View to a Kill.* And Jaclyn Smith turned down the lead role in *Moonraker.*

Episode #74: "Caged Angel"

Written by: B. W. Sandefur
Director: Dennis Donnelly
Airdate: October 31, 1979

Case Plot

After a female inmate is killed during a jewel heist, the girl's father hires the Angels to find out what happened because she was still in prison. Kris shows up at the prison as a transferee. Her juicy background as a manager of a jewelry store catches the eye of Big Aggie and her gang. The gang forces Kris to join them in their next robbery—the jewelry store that Kris worked at. After discovering that the alarm system at the jewelry store has changed, Kelly and Tiffany arrive at the prison, disguised as nuns to provide Kris with updated information. However, Kris's cover is blown when the information about the alarm system is found. As Big Aggie and her gang race to kill her as Kris enlists a fellow inmate for help.

Dyke Villain

Big Aggie is one of those menacing, overweight, ultramean women who like to dominate little women as their playthings. When Kris arrives at the prison, Aggie has eyes only for her. She terrorizes Kris and gives her the name "Poor Little Chicken." Everyone is scared of Big Aggie. Actress Shirley Stoler played the role and was seen in films such as *The Deer Hunter, Klute,* and *Desperately Seeking Susan.*

Gayest Moment

Kris has to strip down and get sprayed as she enters into the prison. She now knows what her sister Jill and coworkers Sabrina and Kelly had to go through at the Pine Parish Prison Farm ("Angels in Chains").

Cherub Guest Star Alert

Sally Kirkland played the dim-witted and kindhearted Lonnie. She is also the inmate who helps Kris fight for her life against Big Aggie and her gang. Kirkland also appeared in "Taxi Angels." Kirkland went on to win the 1998 Golden Globe award for *Anna.*

Tidbit
Former Angel Kate Jackson guest-starred with Lynn Carlin (Warden Ingram) in the pilot episode of "James at 15," in which Jackson plays a hitchhiker that James (Lance Kerwin) meets on his way back home after running away.

Angel Memory: Cheryl Ladd
"I just remember it being fun. I never wanted to go to jail."

Episode #75: "Angels on the Street"

Written by: Edward J. Lakso
Story: Laurie Lakso
Director: Don Chaffey
Airdate: November 7, 1979

Case Plot
After repeated attacks on dance instructor Judy Harkins, the Angels are hired by her father to figure out who would do this to her. After discovering that Freddie the pimp is behind the beatings, Tiffany and Kelly take on the role of streetwalkers. The twosome befriend a hooker named Rose who angrily dislikes Judy. When Freddie suspects that Kelly and Tiffany are undercover cops, he sets them up to be killed. In order to find them, Kris asks for help from Judy, whom she realizes has a split personality, one of whom is Rose.

Tidbit
The Angels do this case pro bono after the client's check bounces.

Gayest Moment

When Tiffany and Kelly tell Bosley their hooker rate is $1,000 apiece, he of course asks why so high, and they let him know that they work as a team Now that's one kinky slice of heaven, any way you look at it!

Episode #79: "Angel Hunt"

Written by: Lee Sheldon
Director: Paul Stanley
Airdate: December 5, 1979

Case Plot

Kris receives a call from a man she believes is Charlie asking her and the Angels to join him in Mazatlán. But after they arrive, they are dropped off on a deserted island filled with dangerous wild animals. The Angels have unknowingly become the hunted game of crazed man Malcolm Case, who blames Charlie for sending him to prison. Malcolm wants payback, so he's taken what Charlie loves the most and uses them as live bait. His ultimate goal is to bring Charlie out of hiding and to kill him.

Gayest Moment

The tender moment between Kris, Kelly, and Tiffany: scared, cold, and hungry, the threesome have some bonding time as Tiffany lets her fellow Angels know how she feels about them.

Spelling Connection

Actor Lloyd Bochner plays the evil game hunter Malcolm Case, who wants to kill off the Angels and hang Charlie's head over his mantel. He also guest-starred in "Angels Belong in Heaven." Bochner went on to play Cecil Colby in Spelling's *Dynasty* and was seen in "To Serve Man," a fan favorite episode of *The Twilight Zone.* He was also nominated for a "Razzie Award" for his work in *The Lonely Lady,* which starred Pia Zadora.

Missing Charlie

The Angels radio Charlie to let him know that they are all okay. Unfortunately, before Kelly can view his face through the binoculars, Charlie's speedboat turns quickly around, allowing Kelly to see only the back of his head. Maybe being so truthful shouldn't always be the best policy, Angels!

One Real Charlie

"Angel Hunt" was one of the few episodes in which we actually "see" Charlie, well, the back side of him. Actor Lou Felder was the lucky actor to play Charlie Townsend in this episode. "People are really impressed when they find out that I played Charlie." On the set, Felder only worked with David Doyle. He eventually worked with Angel Kate Jackson in *Scarecrow and Mrs. King* and Jaclyn Smith in *Christine Cromwell.*

Mega-famous Star Alert—Episode #86: Cesar Romero in "Dancin' Angels"

Airdate: February 6, 1980

Cesar Romero plays Elton Mills, the band director and, oops, the killer! Romero was known for his signature mustache and played the part of the Latin lover in feature films from the 1930s to the 1950s. He was most recognized as the Joker from the TV show *Batman*.

Guest Star Memories

Actor Norman Alden, who guest-starred as P. J. Wilkes, remembered one scary moment on the set when Shelley Hack fainted. "Cast and crew were freaked out for a few moments. Ms. Hack took a moment to recover, and the set was back to dancing and filming."

Lost Angel Episode: "Guardian Angel"

Written by: Bob and Esther Mitchell
Revised Second draft: July 16, 1979

Another episode that was never produced. This case centers around Kris as she befriends a brilliant young scientist named Justin Beaumont Schuyler (JB). When he ends up kidnapped, Kris is contacted by someone who believes she's his mother. After JB gives her clues to his whereabouts, Kris ends up getting caught while trying to rescue him. As they are locked in a supply room, JP builds a bomb, which assists Kelly, Tiffany, and Bosley in locating them after it explodes, hence saving them both and enabling them to nab their captors.

Tidbit

Episodes during the fourth season were structured around one Angel, with the other two providing minimal backup. It was written prior to hiring the new Angel, Tiffany Welles, and gave that new character fewer than ten lines.

Celestial Hunk Alert—Episode #87: Robert Englund in "Harrigan's Angels"

Airdate: February 20, 1980

Robert Englund plays Harold Belkin, a photo engraver who is part of a group robbing an electronics company. Englund went on scare the "Hell" out of teenagers as Freddy Krueger in the 1984 horror classic film, *A Nightmare on Elm Street.* That movie spawned eight feature films and two TV series.

Episode #91: "Toni's Boys"

Written by: Katharyn Powers
Director: Ron Satlof
Airdate: April 2, 1980

Case Plot

Charlie fears for the safety of his Angels after someone makes several attempts to kill them. He brings in Antonia Blake and her "boys," Cotton, Matt, and Bob, to protect them. Soon after they join forces, Tiffany is kidnapped. Kelly and Kris are then used as bait, but the plan backfires when they are abducted. As the Angels are being entombed in a wine cellar, "Toni's Boys" flex their muscles and save the day.

Tidbit

Spelling and Goldberg wanted to make a spin-off of *Charlie's Angels*—their idea was to make a male version of the show. So they cast three sexy studs—an Olympic athlete, a cowboy, and a master of disguise. Cotton Harper (Stephen Shortridge), Bob Sorensen (Bob Seagren), and Matt Parrish (Bruce Bauer) were the three detectives, and they worked for a woman named Antonia "Toni." Blake. (Barbara Stanwyck).

Prior to *Charlie's Angels,* Jaclyn Smith and Bruce Bauer, who plays Matt Parrish, appeared in a TV commercial for Palmolive.

Gayest Moment

Bob Sorensen (Bob Seagren) has to remove his shirt as he interviews to be a drummer in a male strip club. Nice beefcake!

Mega-famous Star Alert

Hollywood legend Barbara Stanwyck played the part of Antonia Blake. Stanwyck was known for her various films, *Ball of Fire, Double Indemnity, Sorry Wrong Number*, and *Stella Dallas*. She became a TV staple with *The Barbara Stanwyck Show* and *The Big Valley* and won Emmys for both. Her final work was on the *Dynasty* spin-off *The Colbys,* as Constance "Conny" Colby Patterson.

Angel Stunt Memory: Bob Seagren, Olympic Gold Medallist for Pole Vaulting

"They hired a high school kid to actually do the jump over the fence into some boxes. They didn't want me to do it, and actually I didn't want to do it either, to be honest with you."

Angel Memory: Jaclyn Smith

"Barbara Stanwyck was exciting. I had been a fan, and all of sudden she's there on the set. She could also be a little intimidating. I do recall we moved our schedules around to shoot all of her close-ups and her scenes first."

Angel Memory: Cheryl Ladd

"Barbara Stanwyck, or Ms. Stanwyck, as we all called her, was a complete pro. We were all just a little bit intimidated by her."

Episodes #92–#93: "One Love . . . Two Angels" (parts 1 and 2)

Written by: B. W. Sandefur
Director: Dennis Donnelly
Airdate: April 30 and May 7, 1980

Case Plot

Kelly is approached by investigator Bill Cord and told that she may be the long-lost daughter of multimillionaire Oliver Barrows. After Barrows is convinced that Kelly is his daughter Margaret, he dies of a heart attack. Kelly hires Tiffany and Kris to find out if she is, in fact, Margaret Ellen Barrows.

During the investigation, Kris and Kelly both fall for Bill Cord. When Kelly almost dies in a car accident, Kris catches Kelly in the arms of Cord, setting up a rift between the two Angels. After Cord mysteriously drowns, Tiffany is left alone to solve the case. In the end, the whole thing was a setup. Barrow's nephew Glenn was manipulating the situation to take control of his estate.

Tidbit

This was Shelley Hack's final episode and was one of the best-written for her character. It was the only episode that aired in two parts when it was originally shown on network TV.

Jaclyn Smith and Cheryl Ladd were pitted against each other once again in 1983, when their respective TV movies *Rage of Angels* and *Grace Kelly* were both aired on the same night at the same time.

Gayest Moment

Kris and Kelly both turn in their resignation letters because they can no longer work together. In the end, they make up and hug, and it is Tiffany that leaves the team.

Celestial Hunk Alert

Patrick Duffy plays the dashing man who falls in love with two Angels. Which Angel would have won his heart, had he not died? Maybe Tiffany, since she had a lot of free time on her hands after she left Charlie's employment. Duffy at the same time was on the long-running TV show *Dallas* as Bobby Ewing. Duffy also did two other successful TV series, *The Man from Atlantis* and *Step by Step.*

Angel Memory: Jaclyn Smith

"Patrick Duffy was so funny."

CELEBRITY SURVEY #4: WHAT IS YOUR FAVORITE *CHARLIE'S ANGELS* EPISODE?

"'Angels in Chains.'"

—John August, screenwriter, *Charlie's Angels, Charlie's Angels: Full Throttle, Go*

"It's been a long time. I'll confess I haven't been watching the show in reruns. but if memory serves, there was a great episode where they went undercover at a beauty pageant, right? That was good television."

—Peter Paige, actor, *Queer as Folk*

"Where they went undercover at a beauty pageant and foiled the bad guy."

—ANT, comedian, actor, *Last Comic Standing*

"Those drugs have erased much of my memory, and of course, I was *so* very young when they aired, but I do recall being thrilled with an episode which featured a criminal female impersonator. Even as a kid, I always loved the nightclub scenes in films or TV. There was some great onstage and dressing room footage, and the queen would don various female disguises to commit its crimes in. And at the 'startling' conclusion, there's a chase which ends with the female mimic falling, and his wig comes off, revealing a sad, whimpering, balding man. If I'm not mistaken, he was a Vietnam vet who had gone psycho."

—Lady Bunny, ladybunny.net

"Yeah. probably won't be very original with this one but the prison episode is probably my favorite. Those cute blue uniforms and all of them chained together? Kind of hot. And maybe the ski episode where they are all hooking up. That was a fun one too. You didn't see them hook up much, so that was cool. Even though I really wanted them to hook up with chicks. Oh, and the one where Charlie gets kidnapped and they have to rescue him from that island. Lots of swimsuits. Ha."

—Michelle Wolff, actress, *Dante's Cove*

"Oh dear, I'm so bad with facts . . . Season 1, Episode 7: 'To Kill an Angel,' original broadcast date November 10, 1976. Kelly gets shot in the head and wanders around an amusement park with a little boy. Genius! I laughed, I cried, I became a drag queen."

—Jackie Beat, jackiebeatrules.com

"'Pretty Angels All in a Row,' but I also love 'Angel on the Street,' where Kelly is a hooker but during the day is a sweet girl that sings. I thought that episode was so hysterical. In *Chico's Angels,* episode three, we parodied that one and combined it with 'Angels in Chains.' We did a whole undercover high school hooker–type story of the poor insane girl who is a big streetwalker at night. That's also one of my favorites just because again, so wrong, here are these beautiful women being hookers and they look nothing like hookers."

—Oscar Quintero, actor, *Chico's Angels*

"'Angels in Chains,' that's definitely the one which sticks out in my mind. I actually did a porno called *Hole Patrol,* which was a take-off of 'Angels in Chains.' Where the boys get arrested for no reason and are thrown in a hick jail and there is a bad warden."

—Chi Chi LaRue, director, Channel 1 Releasing

"'Angels in Chains.' . . . Women in prison, brutal Sapphic guards, a perverse redneck sheriff, forced prostitution with glitzy cocktail dresses, running through reeds chained together, buckets of lip gloss, *and* a young Kim Basinger . . . *What's Not to Love???!*"

—Glen Hanson, artist,
glenhanson.com

"I have an unnatural affection for 'The Sammy Davis Jr. Kidnap Caper,' in which Sammy plays both himself and his obnoxious double who gets kidnapped by mistake. Really, what are the chances of finding two one-eyed black Jews and then mixing them up?"

—Frank DeCaro, host, *The Frank DeCaro Show* on Sirius

"I would have to say 'Pom Pom Angels.' Because I've always been obsessed with being a cheerleader—I wasn't one because I couldn't actually make myself run for cheerleader, it seemed too stupid at the time, and I've always regretted it. But every girl is aware of the power of cheerleaders because the cute, hunky boys can't seem to resist that outfit. So to see all the girls cheering to solve a crime, well, it doesn't get any better. I don't remember the details of the episode (I was a mere child at the time) but the image of them wearing those sex kitten outfits will never leave me."

—Julie Brown, comedian, actress, singer, juliebrown.com

"'Angels on Skates!' The one with the roller-skating heiress who is kidnapped, and one of the Angels has to go undercover, but not Tiffany Welles because she is too tall to be on skates! Maybe spunky Kris, little Farrah Fawcett–Minor. She is so cute. I loved the stunt double for Kris. She was awesome. She looks nothing like her, and the wig was ridiculous. It was a good episode."

—Dylan Vox, actor, *The Lair*

Season Five

Episode #94: "Angel in Hiding"

Written by: Edward J. Lasko
Director: Dennis Donnelly
Airdate: November 30, 1980

Case Plot

Kelly and Kris are manning the office after Tiffany decides to stay back East for a while. Their latest case is to locate Jody Mills, a missing model. As they begin their investigation, they find out she has been murdered. While investigating suspects, they learn that her roommate Julie Rogers has been investigating the case herself with her

The Case File Breakdowns: Season Five, 1980–1981

Angels	*Airtime*	*Final Rating*	*Cost per Episode*
Kelly Garrett Kris Munroe Julie Rogers John Bosley	Sundays, 8 p.m.–9 p.m. (Nov. 16, 1980–Jan. 11, 1981) Saturday, 8 p.m.–9 p.m. (Jan. 1981–Feb. 1981) Wednesdays, 9 p.m.–10 p.m. (June 1981)	47	$650,000

former parole officer Harry Stearns. After Harry is killed, Julie teams up with Kris and Kelly to help catch his killer.

As Kelly and Kris attempt to become models, Kelly does the best that she can, while Kris purposely makes

The fifth and final season of *Charlie's Angels:* the cast with new Angel Tanya Roberts, Jaclyn Smith, and Cheryl Ladd. (© American Broadcasting Companies, Inc.)

mistakes. After falling from grace, Kris ends up at a sleazy photo studio where she runs into a client from the modeling agency. As he begins to question her, she realizes that he is responsible for the death of Jody Mills.

Tidbit

This episode originally premiered as a three-hour movie on November 30, 1980, and introduced the world to Charlie's newest Angel, Tanya Roberts. The episode was originally titled "Street Models and Hawaiian Angels." When the show went into syndication, it was split into three episodes: "Angel in Hiding," parts 1 and 2, and "To See an Angel Die."

Tanya Roberts had previously worked with guest star Dack Rambo in the TV series pilot "Waikiki," about two detectives who are investigating a serial killer in Hawaii. Roberts was one of the killer's victims.

Gayest Moment

Bosley introduces Julie to Kris and Kelly as their new partner in crime solving: a glamorous model turned private investigator. Yep, that's believable!

Mega-famous Star Alert

Actor Vic Morrow plays Lt. Harry Stearns, the man who was Julie Roger's mentor. He also appeared in "Angels in Vegas." In 1982, while filming *Twilight Zone: The Movie,* Morrow was killed in a freak helicopter accident. He is survived by his daughter, actress Jennifer Jason Leigh.

Mega-famous Star Alert—Episode #95: Jane Wyman in "To See an Angel Die"

Airdate: November 30, 1980

Jane Wyman portrays psychic Eleanor Willard, who discovers that Kris has been kidnapped and senses that Kris's life is in danger. Wyman was the first wife of President Ronald Reagan. She won the 1949 Oscar for Best Actress in a Leading Role in *Johnny Belinda.* And in 1981 she joined the nighttime soap opera *Falcon Crest,* playing Angela Channing.

Angel Memory: Tanya Roberts

"I was a big fan of Jane Wyman. She was fantastic, and it was a great honor to work with her."

"I remember the day we went shopping for bathing suits. There was a bathing suit shop south of Wilshire and Beverly. I was in there for eight hours!"

—Tanya Roberts

TOP TEN BATHING SUITS

Bathing suits were the sexiest part of the series. Each Angel was seen in bathing attire at least once, with the exception of Sabrina. Maybe if Nolan Miller could have created a turtleneck swimsuit, she would have worn one. Here are the top ten best moments:

1. "Pilot," "The Killing Kind," and "Night of the Strangler": Kelly Garrett in that famous white bikini.
2. "The Mexican Connection": Jill Munroe found herself swimming in a sexy peach one-piece suit.
3. "The Mexican Connection": Kelly wearing her bottoms-up bathing suit in which she always gets proposals, but never of marriage.
4. "Angels at Sea": Sabrina's only reference to a bathing suit, when she tells the other Angels that her bikini had been burned in her cabin fire.
5. "Angels in Paradise": Rescuing Charlie is hard work, especially in the sexy bikinis Kelly and Kris are wearing.

Celestial Hunk Alert—Episode #96: Sony Bono in "Angel of the Deep"

Airdate: December 7, 1980

Sonny Bono plays a hippie named Walrus who is trying to sell "Maui Wowie" (marijuana) to airline stewardess Cindy Lee. Bono is best known for his singing partnership with and marriage to gay icon Cher. *The*

6. "Pretty Angels all in a Row": Kris showing up in a provocative bikini. She is sure to win the Miss Chrysanthemum title! Hi, there. *Hello!*
7. "Angels on High": Kris's bikini was so tiny that they had to pull in the frame to keep from exposing most of her. Ladd got in a bit of trouble with producer Aaron Spelling for wearing that bikini and was called the "Little Rebel."
8. "Love Boat Angels": Whether wearing green bikini to match her grasshopper or white to show off her innocence, Kris's bikinis knew how to grab attention. Not to mention Doc, Gopher, and Isaac—the Love Boat cast couldn't keep their eyes off her either!
9. "Love Boat Angels": Tiffany is in a one-piece pink bathing suit, which makes her maiden voyage a true success.
10. "Angels of the Deep": This is the first time in the series that all three Angels were in bikinis at the same time. Now that really is heaven!

Sonny and Cher Show ruled the TV variety hour from 1973 to 1978. Bono went on to become the mayor of Palm Springs, California, and then a Congressman from the state of California. Bono died in 2001 in a fatal skiing accident.

Angel Memory: Tanya Roberts
"Sonny was fun, sweet and friendly."

Celestial Hunk Alert—Episode #97: Lyle Waggoner in "Island Angels"

Airdate: December 14, 1980

Lyle Waggoner portrays Jack Barrows, an adulterer who is having an affair with assassin Lisa Gallo (Carol Lynley). Waggoner is best known for appearing on the *Carol Burnett Show.* He is also well known for playing Steve Trevor on the hit Lynda Carter TV series, *Wonder Woman.* And in 1973, he posed nude for *Cosmopolitan* magazine.

Cherub Guest Star Alert—Episode #97: Barbi Benton in "Island Angels"

Airdate: December 14, 1980

Barbi Benton plays sexy Toni Green, the bubbly social director of the swinging singles. Benton is well known for gracing the pages of *Playboy* and/or being the girlfriend of Hugh Hefner throughout the 1960s and 1970s. She went on to become a *Hee Haw* honey and was a regular guest star on various Aaron Spelling shows.

Episode #99: "Hula Angels"

Written by: Robert George

Director: Kim Manners

Airdate: January 11, 1981

Case Plot

Steve Moss, a successful nightclub owner, is kidnapped and held for a $1 million ransom. Each night Steve's wife is unable to pay the money, a different dancer disappears. As the Angels come in to investigate, Julie and Kris audition as replacement dancers. After becoming suspicious of the choreographer, Kris sets herself up to be the next victim. However, her plan backfires when they take Julie instead. Upon Charlie's suggestion, the Angels set up a fake money drop to expose the kidnappers and lead them back to Julie and Steve.

Tidbit

Due to the SAG actors strike, this was the final episode filmed in Hawaii. It is also the last episode in which the Angels wear swimsuits. Upon returning to Los Angeles, they turn in their bikinis for sweaters.

This is the second episode in which Gene Barry guest-stars. He also appears in "Angels in the Wings" (episode 32).

Gayest Moment

Kris and Julie go-go dance to their heart's content while perched in a bird cage. No wonder these Angels wanted to fly the coop!

Cherub Guest Star Alert

Joanna Cassidy plays bad girl Stacy Parrish, the mastermind behind the kidnappings. Cassidy is a very accomplished actor, with such hit films as *Blade Runner, Who Framed Roger Rabbit*, and *Don't Tell Mom the Babysitter's Dead*. On TV she costarred in *Buffalo Bill*, for which she also won a Golden Globe, and most recently guest-starred in *Boston Legal* as the love interest for William Shatner.

Angel Semi-Regular

Soon-Tek Oh played Lt. Torres, and is the Angels' police contact while working on the islands. And in the 1990s, Oh made a guest appearance on Cheryl Ladd's TV series, *One West Waikiki.*

Angel Memory: Tanya Roberts

"During this episode we were caught in the cage swinging above the ground, and after shooting they actually could not get the cage open!"

Drag Queen Alert—Episode #103: "Angel on the Line"

Written by: Edward J. Lasko
Director: Kim Manners
Airdate: February 14, 1981

Case Plot

At a singles club, patrons make contact with each other via telephones placed at their tables. After a woman is threatened, she hastily leaves and is hit by an oncoming vehicle. The Angels hit the nightclub scene to probe into her death. Upon arriving at the club, Kelly's "perfect pretty face" attracts unwanted attention, and she is targeted as the stalker's next victim. At the end of the evening, Kelly speaks with Margo, the hypnotist, about the woman who was killed.

The next day, Kelly is approached by a stranger who tracked her down through Margo and claims to have seen her at the club the night before. Treating her to lunch, he proceeds to tell her how pretty she is. Later that afternoon, Kelly returns to the club to meet up with Margo. After briefly discussing the stranger, Margo forces Kelly back behind the club, where she attacks her. During the attack, Kelly realizes that Margo and the stranger are the same person. Now that's a drag!

Tidbit

This is the only episode that features a female impersonator. I know many drag queens who would kill to be an Angel, but this is ridiculous.

Alley Cat Alert

Margo goes up against Kelly with a switchblade. Heel to heel, claw to claw. It's all over for Margo when her makeup runs after she slips face-first into a mud puddle.

Episode #104: "Chorus Line Angels"

Written by: Edward J. Lasko
Director: David Doyle
Airdate: February 21, 1981

Case Plot

A Vegas-bound musical is riddled with problems after the show's choreographer goes missing and lead dancer walks out. One of the show's financial backers hires the Angels to find out the source of the problems. Kelly dusts off her dancing shoes, with Julie taking on the role of her manager, and Kris poses as a reporter. The Angels eventually discover that the producer's goal was to have the show fail so that he could pocket all the investors' money.

Tidbit

David Doyle sat in the director's chair for this episode, making him the only cast member to direct during the show's five-year run.

Gayest Moment

A musical is gay enough! The show is no *Phantom of the Opera* or *Wicked,* but anything to do with the stage we just *love*! The catchy tune, "We'll Be Friends to the End," is the big musical number and is great no matter how many times you hear it!

Cherub Guest Star Alert

Lee Travis played one of the heavenly dancers in this episode. She also appeared in "Angel Flight," "Angels in Vegas," and "Love Boat Angels." She is married to producer Edward J. Lakso, who produced and wrote many episodes in this series.

Angel Memory: Jaclyn Smith

"David was a fun director. He knew what he was doing, and he certainly knew our characters. He could pull things out of us as actors, more so than other directors."

Angel Memory: Tanya Roberts

"David was a great director and very helpful."

Episode #108: "Mr. Galaxy"

Written by: Mickey Rich
Story by: Larry Mitchell, Robert Spears
Director: Don Chaffey
Airdate: June 17, 1981

Case Plot

Several murder attempts have been made on Ron Gates, a candidate in the "Mr. Galaxy" competition. The Angels take on the highly competitive world of bodybuilding. Their number 1 suspect is mobster Danny Barr, the owner of a training gym. The Angels come to the conclusion that Danny wants to get Ron out of the competition so his contender can continue his winning streak.

Gayest Moment

Big, beefy, oiled-up hunks in Speedos—need we say more?

Celestial Hunk Alert

Roger Callard, who plays Ron Gates, was a well-known bodybuilder in the late 1970s. He won Mr. USA in 1975, Mr. America in 1977, and then Mr. International in 1978.

Episode #109: "Let Our Angel Live" (final episode)

Written by: Edward J. Lakso
Director: Kim Manners
Airdate: June 24, 1981

Case Plot

As Kelly confronts a suspected embezzler, he shoots her in the head with a concealed gun. She is rushed off to the hospital in critical condition. While she is in surgery, Kris, Julie, and Bosley reminisce about their past cases together. Eventually Kelly pulls through, and they find out that Charlie was by her side all throughout the operation.

Tidbit

When reminiscing, Kris reminds Bosley about the last time they were in that hospital together. However, the episode she is referring to is "Terror on Ward One (episode #18) from the first season before she joined the team. Who knows, maybe Jill told her the story!

Gayest Moment

Kelly's perfect makeup while in surgery. It once again proves that even if you get shot in the head, you can still look your all-time best. Thanks, Max!

Missing Charlie

While in surgery, Kelly hears Charlie's voice but is unable to make out his face. And this is the first time that Charlie's eyes are revealed, as he looks over the Angels in the final scene.

Angel Memory: Tanya Roberts

"One time, during filming of one of the episodes, I got into a car and it turned out it was not a part of the show! There I was in a stranger's car."

CLOSE-UP

Heavenly Chat with Beefcake Angel Bob Seagren, Episode #91: "Toni's Boys"

Everybody gets their hopes up when you think you're going to get a spin-off for a new series, and when it doesn't happen, it's a little bit of a letdown. Coming out of athletics and winning an Olympic medal, I got into show business and people started calling, "Hey, you ever thought about acting?" and how I had never given it a second thought. So I started doing commercials and then little walk-on roles. All the episodic shows, and went on from there. I had done a few guest spots on a few Aaron Spelling shows. I went in and read and ended up getting the part. I had done two episodes of *Fantasy Island* for Spelling prior, and we read for this, and of course it was supposed to be a spin-off of a new series of three guys. That was pretty exciting at the time. Of course with a name like Barbara Stanwyck playing the David Doyle part, at the time that was pretty huge.

It came down to the wire; they ended up with three guys, me, Stephen Shortridge, and Bruce Bauer. So we were pretty excited and had high hopes; we knew it was going to run as a special one-hour episode of *Charlie's Angels* and see how the rating go, if it was going to be spun off or not. Anyway, it never did. I don't even know how the ratings were. But it never made it.

Working with Barbara Stanwyck was interesting. Here she is a legend and she couldn't have been nicer. She was so sweet, very charming, and very personable. She had her lines and she was there to work, to get it down and no messing around.

Barbara Stanwyck was one very professional women. She got a little bit fried over the combing out of the Angels' hair, when everyone was ready to act. I remember, because I was pretty green, I didn't know what was going on, but I could see she was getting very upset. You block out a scene; everybody would leave and go back to their trailers. Then they call you to shoot, and everybody is standing there ready to shoot, and of course it's twenty more minutes while the girls are having their hair combed out again. Barbara apparently made a comment and was complaining that this was very unprofessional and to do that in your trailer. I remember she came back the next day, first take; we started to shoot, the girls came out, and twenty minutes of comb and hair. All of a sudden I saw Barbara: she was sitting at a desk in the shot. She politely folded the desk calendar and gets up and walks away. She left. Of course, everybody is just in panic mode. So everything shut down for half the day, because Barbara Stanwyck got in her limo and left. Poor Aaron Spelling. I don't know how it was, really pleading and begging, then of course it was, "Brush your hair in your trailer. You walk on the set to be ready to shoot." The pace picked up after that, but it gradually went back to its old ways.

All the Angels are gorgeous-looking women, and of course Farrah Fawcett I think turned some heads and launched the show. I had the opportunity to work with Kate on *Scarecrow and Mrs. King* and Jaclyn in *Windmills of the Gods.* But being paired up with Cheryl Ladd on the episode was sort of ironic, because our kids went to school together. Jordan (Ladd) and my daughter are the same age and were in the same class at Curtis School. It was sort of a coincidence to be paired up with her.

I don't even remember taking off my shirt! I didn't think about it at the time. Obviously you knew it was three guys cheesecake. You're not dumb; you know what they are trying to sell. That was the flattering part: they picked three guys that are put into the shoes of three beautiful women. That was very flattering to be selected for that.

Thank you for visiting Charles Townsend
Private Investigations.
The agency has three locations: Los Angeles,
Hawaii, and Paris.

Our LA office is located at 193 Robertson Boulevard.,
Beverly Hills, California.
The phone numbers is 213-555-0267, and the private
line is 213-555-9626.

If you are visiting Hawaii, we are located at
4376 Kahaii Avenue, Honolulu, Hawaii.

CALL IF YOU NEED US!

Acknowledgments

I need to send a thousand heavenly thank-yous to Cheryl Ladd, who is my true Angel. You have been so kind to me for so many years! No wonder so many years ago, I chose you as my favorite angel!

Farrah Fawcett, thank you for being a dear friend and a real-life Angel. I hope we will be friends to the end! . . . and YES, you did GOOD! Kiss and love always.

To the free-spirited and angelic Tanya Roberts—thank you for doing my foreword and sharing your angelic memories! You're the best girl!

To the timeless beauty, Jaclyn Smith, thank you for taking time during your horrible cold to chat with me! You're a heavenly angel all the time! Thanks a million halos!

To the man behind all things *Charlie's Angels,* Leonard Goldberg. Your show has brought me so many years of great joy and a bit of fame. Thank you for being so kind to me all these years!

Heavenly thank-you shout-outs to Kate Jackson, Shelley Hack, David Doyle, and John Forsythe. Your work on the show has brought me years of enjoyment.

Thanks to the late, great Aaron Spelling for making my TV so wonderful with *Charlie's Angels* and my other Spelling favorites: *Hart to Hart, Fantasy Island, The Love Boat, Melrose Place, Savannah,* and *Charmed*!

Thanks to Dale Cunningham, Paul Florez, and the entire staff at Alyson Books for allowing me to share my love for all things *Charlie's Angels* with the world again!

A special thank-you to Joe Pittman, who brought me to the Alyson Books family.

To the man with the golden hairdryer, José Eber! A million thank-yous for your hair tips and just being your fabulous self! Thanks, Darling!

Thanks to Oscar Quintero for dressing up Charlie's Angels in laughter with your Latin style!

Cloud of thank-yous to all my guest-star interviewees: Kres Mersky, Bo Hopkins, Brian Cutler, Audrey Landers, Judy Landers, Harvey Jason, Bob Seagren, Norman Alden and Lou Felder. It was an honor for me to chat with you about your Angel experiences!

Big kisses and thank-yous to all the celebrities who took my survey! John August, Peter Paige, ANT, Lady Bunny, Michelle Wolff, Jackie Beat, Chi Chi LaRue, Glen Hanson, Miss Coco Peru, Frank DeCaro, Julie Brown, and Dylan Vox. You all reminded me why I loved *Charlie's Angels* so much!

Special personal thank-you to Scott Jonson, who worked tirelessly on making my words sound great. Words can't thank you enough. Thanks.

A thank-you to Joey Marshall for his untapped knowledge of all the episodes. Your memory is so captivating!

The warmest Angel thank you to Glen Hanson for his wonderful rendition of Charlie's Angels for the cover of the book! It's been all the talk of the "Angel" fan community!

Thanks to Coral Petretti at ABC Archive Photo, Cynthia A. Lai, and Nancy Barr-Brandon for all the great images.

Shout-outs to my friends who always put up with me: Brian Lamberson, Charlene Tilton, Jules Massey, Julie Fick, Eric T., , Ellen Loughlin, Monica Holmes, and the Hacienda crew: Chris Kosloski, Shaun Neale, Josh Griffith, Dawn Robinson, and Morgan Slate.

Big Angel kisses to my sister Elizabeth and her husband Rob and my coolest nephews, Jamison and Kendrick!

. . . and to my parents, once again, to whom this book is dedicated. I love you both!

—Mike